D1461605

Author ....

Title .... Words, words, words

.... Stock no. 57016643

This item should be returned or brought in for renewal
by the last date stamped below

28 NOV 1987

-3. NOV. ...7

-1 FEB 2008

WITHDRAWN

19 AUG 2024

WITHDRAWN

19 AUG 2024

TELEPEN

57016643

Polonius	*What do you read, my lord?*
Hamlet	*Words, words, words*

WORDS
WORDS
WORDS

C.M. Matthews

LUTTERWORTH PRESS
Guildford and London

First published 1979

ISBN 0 7188 2341 9

Printed in Great Britain by Butler & Tanner Ltd
Frome and London

To
CAROLA
another word lover

Contents

NOTE   *The illustrations appear on pages 66–71.*

List of Illustrations

Acknowledgements

The author and the publishers would like to thank those who have granted permission for the reproduction of copyright illustrations in this book. Figure 1 is reproduced by kind permission of the President and Fellows of Corpus Christi College, Oxford; Figures 2 and 4 by kind permission of the British Museum; Figure 3 by kind permission of Lambeth Palace Library. The copy of Dr Johnson's *Dictionary of the English Language* was kindly lent by Mr Robert Boyle. The photograph of Sir James Murray, which appears in the biography written by his grand-daughter, Miss K. M. E. Murray, *Caught in a Web of Words*, published by Yale University Press, is reproduced with the kind permission of Miss Murray and Yale University Press.

The author and the publishers would also like to thank J. M. Dent & Sons Ltd and the Trustees for the Copyrights of the late Dylan Thomas for permission to quote the lines from *Fern Hill*, taken from the *Collected Poems* of Dylan Thomas.

I

THE QUESTION

Human beings are talkative creatures and always have been, so far as we can see. It was our urge to communicate with each other and growing ability to do so that was probably the chief factor in the development that made us different from all other animals. Leading anthropologists are now of the opinion that it was not so much aggressiveness as ability to co-operate that gave the earliest forms of man a superiority over others of the ape family, and co-operation entails communication.

As far back as 750,000 years ago some primitive men, or hominids, had mastered the use of fire. This signified a great mental advance for it is natural to all animals to fear fire, and only by combining together, passing on acquired knowledge, and making plans could men conquer this fear and turn what had been a cause of terror to their own advantage. All this signifies that already they had language of a sort.

There are other means of communication besides speech —grimaces, smells, gestures and movements of all sorts; bees we are told convey detailed information by means of a kind of dance, and we too show our feelings by many visible signs, but it is the spoken word, developed to an extraordinary degree of precision and variation, that has distinguished man from the rest of creation in every part of the world where he has strayed.

Most of the animals make meaningful noises but their range is strictly limited. 'Danger', 'Keep still', 'Go away', or 'Where are you?' are some of the messages that various squawks, squeals, growls and howls have signified through the ages, but useful though they are, they have probably remained unchanged for hundreds of thousands of years,

1

while some creatures like the silly cuckoo have been repeating just one thing all that time.

Men wanted to say more, much more, and this they did wherever they went. Unfortunately there can be no measurable evidence of their progress in this respect, for words are but breath and leave no trace until the invention of writing can give them permanence. The earliest known writing dates from about 4,000 BC and men had been talking for thousands of years before that. Anthropologists can date the mental advance of primitive men only by the measurements of their skulls which 80,000 years ago were exactly the same as our own, and by the enduring artefacts that they left behind them, many of which are far older. But we can be certain that as soon as they were using their brains to make tools and decorations they were also making words.

The beginnings must have been slow just as the making of the first tools was slow. Hundreds of thousands of years for mastering the use of stone, bone, wood and flint, and the first discovered metals, then a gradual quickening of tempo leading to the crescendo of mechanisation in which we now live. So with words. Slow progress at first while the possibilities of throat, tongue, palate and lips were explored and practised, but the more information men found they could impart to each other in this way, the more they wanted to go on doing it. Whether it is tools and gadgets or words and speeches, man is never satisfied. He always wants more, and what he wants he makes.

Fluent and efficient speech is common to all mankind however isolated or backward in other respects; no race so primitive but has been found to possess an elaborate spoken language. The Australian aborigines who until recently were living in a Stone Age culture with fewer material possessions than any other known people—no houses, no clothes, no flocks or herds—had yet a variety of languages in which they passed on the complicated stories of their rich mythology. So also the Bushmen of Africa who combine extreme

2

material poverty with a wealth of words and unwritten literature.

So man has made words, millions of them, in several thousand languages. The number of languages in the world can't be exactly counted because there is no standard line of demarcation between distinctive dialects and separate languages, but the calculation varies between 2,500 and 4,000. This book is concerned with English only. But English comprises nearly half a million words as assembled in the *Oxford English Dictionary*, the largest vocabulary of any language.

Of course nobody knows all the words in the OED. Some are obsolete, some archaic, and a vast number are technical and scientific terms known only to experts in each particular field. Many more are completely alien words that have won their places as denoting exotic flora or fauna or commodities that English speakers in remote lands call by their native names. A large number are what you might call variations on a theme: if you count hope, hopeful, hopefully, hopelessly, hopelessness, and so on, all as separate words, it soon adds up. However, man deserves credit for his ingenuity in making one word into eight or ten more, each expressing something different. One way and another, no one will deny the vast multiplicity of English words. The choice before us when we open our mouths is far more than we ever make full use of. The average man—we are told—uses only four or five thousand words in his normal speech, though he understands a great many more when he hears or reads them. Shakespeare used over twenty thousand, but again it is a calculation that can't be made exactly, for how can anyone decide what is one word or two? Is heart-ache one or two? Is a noun, such as dream, a different word from the verb in all its forms? But why try to adjudicate? We can agree that he made better use of the language than anyone else, and yet there were not so many words in it then as there are now.

For still we go on making them. The OED is now in the process of bringing out a supplement which when finished

3

is expected to add another 72,000 words, more than half of them scientific. New discoveries and inventions, new ideas and fashions, new social problems and—alas—new crimes, all demand them, and the wonder is that they are always forthcoming. We may run short of fuel, food and water, but never of words.

Where do they come from? How do we find so many? What is the unfailing source, the inexhaustible mine from which we can always produce more? That is the theme of this book. I take it up boldly because one of the pleasant things about words is that they belong to all of us. No government can control them (unless we are exceptionally offensive, which I do not propose to be), charge for them, tax them or ration them. They are ours to enjoy and that is what I mean to do.

I shall not linger in the realms of pre-history. My chief concern is with words as they are now, to see how we are treating them and to ask where and how we got them. But the answers may lie far in the past or in other lands, and that amazing work of scholarship the OED, especially in its noble full-length edition, beckons us back so invitingly that it is easy to slip through the centuries and see the words we are using so casually today as they were in earlier contexts and sometimes strange ones. I shall go where the words lead me.

English has been spoken in England for about fifteen hundred years, in the last three hundred of which it has spread around the world. The tribes of Angles and Saxons with some Jutes who invaded Britain in the fifth century AD had previously spoken it in northern Europe in several dialects which did not differ greatly from each other. All were part of an earlier Germanic tongue which was itself descended from a prehistoric parent language which scholars have named Indo-European, because from it almost all the languages of Europe and some of Asia have branched off. In their new homeland the speech of these tribes merged together in one language which they all called English (*Anglisc* or *Englisc*)

4

and what we call Anglo-Saxon, or more correctly Old English to about 1100.

The first written records of this language date from the eighth century, both in prose and poetry. The prose is brief and business-like at first, but the poetry fluent and prolific. We find our language—for it is our language though it looks baffling to those who haven't studied it—as already expressive and vigorous with a highly complicated grammar and a vocabulary quite sufficient for its needs. Each race creates words to suit itself. Eskimos have over twenty words for different types of snow. The early English had about as many for varying kinds of woodland. We still have a good choice, though some, like holt and hurst, shaw and wold, are obsolete except in place-names. In certain subjects that they loved to talk of, such as courage in battle, adventures on the sea, and loyalty to their chiefs, there was in Old English a profusion of words to choose from.

So we are able to watch the language for a whole millennium since it was first written to the present day, except for a break just after the Norman Conquest when it was driven underground for a time. It emerged again in the thirteenth century changed by the experience and still changing, and at this transitional stage halfway between ancient and modern we call it Middle English. It was still basically the same language and full of life, especially in poetry.

During that thousand years in which the language is spread before us, the chief changes have been a simplification of grammar and a vast growth of vocabulary. Many of the earlier words have been lost along the way but the additions far outnumber those that have gone. We can see how words have been produced whenever wanted, changed to fit changing conditions, shortened, lengthened, chopped up, stuck together, overworked or neglected, but mostly used and used again. And we can deduce that from the time man first began to speak in prehistoric times he has been doing much the same thing.

5

We can see that the two main sources for new words are
either to make them by re-arranging old material we
already have, or else to borrow them from other languages.
In either case we are using second-hand material, or third-
or fourth-hand, but we do it so ingeniously that the result
is often like a new creation. Both methods depend on there
being a stock of old words to play with—or rather many
stocks if we are going to dip into foreign word-banks as well
as our own. The first words were truly original creations.
These are far back in pre-history beyond our reach, but the
art of making them hasn't entirely left us and we can best
begin by thinking how some of these fresh creations can still
come into being.

II

ORIGINAL WORDS

1 Echoes from Nature

The most basic and primitive way of making words, one that we still practise but that must surely be the oldest of all, is by imitating the sounds of nature. The Greeks called this onomatopoeia, but it is simpler to speak of these words as echoic—Greek again.

Every possible sound whether made by birds, animals, insects, inanimate objects, or by man himself has its special word: screech, squeal, cluck, howl, hiss, buzz, clatter, splash, crash, swish, squelch, crunch, thud, creak, mutter, murmur, whisper, shriek, rumble, hubbub, and so on for ever. Modern machines can hardly be called 'nature' but they make noises and we have words for them too, such as zoom, judder, bleep. There must be hundreds of these imitative words, and we never hesitate to coin a new one if ever we feel in need of it. 'It came down on the water with a great sloosh,' you might say, not knowing or caring if there was such a word in the dictionary.

Many living creatures are named from their cries. Obvious examples are the cuckoo, the peewit, and the crow (earlier, the craw). But most of them were named so long ago that sound-changes over the centuries have obscured the origin. As with pictograms which began as representations of objects and were gradually simplified to a few strokes which became symbols for sounds, so the words that have come down to us from remote times must differ greatly from their earliest forms. And yet the name of the bear (OE *bera*) is very close to the 'B–r–r' that one might use still to represent its growl, and it is only in modern times that the English have ceased to roll their 'r's. The name of the wolf, too, which like that of the bear was used by our forefathers in northern Europe long before they came to Britain, had always—as far back as it can be traced—that long -oo- sound (now grown shorter) which, following the rounded 'w', echoes the creature's howl, w-o-o-lf.

How men found words for elemental concepts such as night and day, the sun and the moon, and so forth, is beyond our reach, but can we detect an echoic sound in the word 'wind' with its hollow-sounding 'w' and resonant 'n'? It is an ancient word, as one would expect, not descended from the Latin *ventus* (remember that the Latin 'v' was pronounced 'w') but cognate with it; that is, descended from the same earlier source. Many such ancestral words must have been spoken by the Stone Age hunters of eastern Europe before they divided into separate nations.

A word that certainly grew out of a natural sound is thunder. Before they came into Britain the forbears of the English named one of their principal gods by this sound. They called him Thunor, and imagined him all-powerful as he shook the sky with his rumbling. We know this god better by the shorter form of his name as used by the Scandinavians, Thor. But the Old English form *thunor* was used also as a common noun and in due course acquired the 'd' in the middle which made the sound of it even better.

Then think of Thor's tool, the hammer. This word has exactly the sound of a heavy object that strikes something with a loud *wham*. And what about that other primitive tool, the axe? Isn't its name (which, like hammer, has hardly altered in a thousand years and probably much longer) exactly right for the noise that is made when someone *hacks*? Far more words are based on these echoic sounds than we ever stop to think of.

Some words seem to have come from facial expressions. You can hardly say snarl or sneer without making the appropriate face and the same is true of smirk. Another of this sort is smile, which was formerly pronounced smeel. Smile reminds one of laugh which in its modern form is not particularly suggestive of laughter. But look at the verb to laugh in Old English, *hlæhhan*. 'Hl' was a common combination for starting a word, the 'h' being strongly sounded. The next 'h', coming as it does after a vowel, was like the 'ch' in loch (a sound that remains as 'gh' in many modern words and is now either silent or sometimes pronounced as 'f'). Then comes another 'h' to start the final syllable. Now try *hlæhhan* again with all three 'h's in action and you will find it much more hilarious.

But to return to facial expressions. The combination 'sn' at the beginnings of words is strongly connected with the nose. Apart from sneer and snarl just mentioned, we have sniff, snivel, snuffle, snigger, snout, snort, snore, sneeze and a good many more. With some of them we seem to be wrinkling our noses in distaste. Men have never liked snakes, and the word sneak suggests the same kind of stealthy movement. To snoop is also unpleasant, so also the epithet snide. Both come from America but were nurtured in the same tradition. Snob is first recorded as a slang word for a cobbler—a usage for which no explanation is known—but I have no doubt that it is its first two sounds that have given it the much better-known meaning of a person who turns up his nose at others and is disliked for it, and the same idea is expressed in the more recent snooty. These modern coinages show how very much alive are some of these old associations of sounds and ideas.

Another combination of letters that must once have been expressive of some physical action is 'wr'. This comes from the remoter past and we have no feeling for it now, for the 'w' in this arrangement has long been silent and we make little of the 'r'. To sound the 'w' and roll the 'r' requires quite an effort, and effort—a somewhat violent and angry one—is what the original sound would seem to convey. You wrestle with your enemy and wrest his power from him. Then you can wreak your wrath on him. Wreak, which is now nearly obsolete, is a key word, for something on which the fury of men or the elements has been wreaked becomes a wreck, and a person who has suffered this treatment is wretched. We may describe him as a wretch, but it is illogical that the word should have become derogatory, for according to its etymology a wretch has been a victim rather than a villain.

Many of the wr- words have a sense of twisting and turning—writhe, wreathe, wriggle, wrangle, wrench, wring. Something that has been wrung is wrong, that is to say twisted or distorted, and a crooked thing is wry. A wrist is a joint with remarkable ability to twist, and no doubt writing when first practised by scratching on wood, clay or stone seemed a tortuous affair. To wrap is harmless but does involve winding round.

Something that has been wrought—iron, for instance—has had considerable effort expended on it. Wrought is the old irregular past tense of the verb to work (OE *wyrcan*), which belonged to the same group of words, only in this case a vowel developed between the 'w' and the 'r', rather changing its character.

It may be that this 'wr' sound began with the involuntary grunt a man might make in a strong physical effort, and once it had developed into a word, others of the same sort followed, each slightly varying the sound and sense.

Yet another initial combination of sounds expressive of a special kind of movement—this one light and airy—is 'fl'. Fly, flit, float, flutter. It is hard to say why it should be so, but there it is. Float is a near relation of flow, and other 'fl' words have followed through the centuries with various endings suited to different movements. Flip, flap, flop: how nicely they are graded, the first so light and delicate, the next more strenuous, the last unsuccessful. And still we go on creating new effects for new situations. When plastic sandals became flip-flops a word was coined in an age-old tradition.

There are some words which, without being echoes of

sounds, do seem to express their subjects to perfection in a way that is perfectly clear to us but not easy to explain. Why are toddle and waddle so exactly right for a funny and inexpert kind of walk? And why is twaddle so obviously silly? Why does anything ending in -ump sound so heavy and lumpish? It may be that it started with a true echo of sound in thump, and then what has fallen lies inert making a lump or hump or dump. Bump contains both ideas, the sound and the swelling.

Why are prick, stick, pick, pike and spike all so sharp and prickly, and pillow so soft and gentle in comparison? It isn't all association of ideas: 'k' has a very sharp sound and 'l' a soft one. Lull is a marvellously soothing word.

But it is useless to pretend that this kind of word-making is rational. We can only observe in human beings a creative instinct that causes them to match sounds to things, and then when they have a word that pleases them, to make more on the same pattern but with variations.

We may notice also that the taste for rhyming the ends of words is more recent in English than the habit of repeating initial sounds. Rhymes are almost unknown in Anglo-Saxon poetry in which the chief cause of pleasure to the ear, apart from rhythm, lay in regular alliteration. (For an example, see Appendix 1.) Thus the hump/lump/dump type of word-making is comparatively modern, or at least post-Conquest, while the groups that are linked by the same beginnings (like fl-, wr- and so on) have descended to us from an unknown antiquity. In spite of this, the tendency to make new words this way is far from dead.

2   Fresh Creations

It is not to be supposed that all the oldest words began through the copying of natural noises. It must often have happened that sounds became associated with objects by mere chance or we should not have such a great variety from one language to another. The making of the first words in any language can only be a matter for speculation, but there is one way in which we can study the most primitive attempts at speech at first hand; that is by observing babies.

A baby is an entirely primitive person. In him (by which I mean either sex and no offence intended) we see the instincts, desires and capabilities of the human animal in a natural state, and surely his earliest efforts to communicate by sound must teach us something of how primitive man started on the same course. Three things common to all mankind emerge plainly in any normal baby: first his wish to communicate, secondly his tendency to copy, and thirdly his satisfaction in making noises for their own sake. The earliest noise, crying, is involuntary, instinctive, beyond his control. But by six months old he is making noises deliberately and with the pleasure of a creative artist. You may hear him practising his ba-ba-ba's and gug-gugs happily in his cot when you perhaps would prefer silence. Of course at an early stage his family puts him firmly on the path of attaching certain sounds to certain objects in accordance with their own ideas, and he is wonderfully quick to learn. But were all such influence removed and babies cared for only by deaf mutes (which heaven forbid), there can be no doubt that they would still themselves make a variety of noises and in time attach special meanings to many of them.

Indeed, it is certain that if a group of babies were brought up together in this way they would evolve some sort of elementary language. Not a good one—an efficient language takes thousands of years to grow—but they would establish enough sounds intelligible to each other to get along with.

12

Some of their words would be imitations of sounds they heard other than human voices, and some would come by chance. Supposing one child was shouting 'Gagag' while clutching a certain toy, and another who wanted it shouted the same thing as he tried to grab it, and others joined in, that toy could easily become a gagag to all of them.

In some such chancy way some of the earliest root-words must have been established, and whether they came from copying the sounds of nature or sounds made by other people, the art of imitation played a large part in the process.

But do we still sometimes make words out of nothing but meaningless noise? I suppose we do, especially in small intimate groups like families where we can have our own private jokes, but in the world at large hardly at all, because there is such a vast store of known words to play about with. It is far easier and more effective to dish up what we already have in a new guise, taking advantage of the associations that have grown around it, than to create something entirely new. Occasionally it may be done, generally in a heated moment when annoyance or surprise causes the regular supply of words to fail and some unplanned inspiration fills the gap. 'I was absolutely flummoxed,' someone must have exclaimed for the first time, and it was so good that others repeated it. Flabbergasted is rather of the same ilk, but here we can detect influences from other words, such as feeling flabby because something is ghastly. (But flabby itself has no known origin unless it is a variant of flappy.) Most of the apparently original coinages of the last few centuries do owe something to older words.

In this field of creating new words one must inevitably think of Lewis Carroll and Edward Lear, both of whom did it deliberately for fun. We enjoy their efforts but few of them have attained any real currency in the language. Chortle and galumphing are both very expressive and can be used, but we have no occasion to speak of a slithy tove, or even a Jabberwock, except as typical of invented creatures.

Again, with Lear we love his Pobble, his Dong and his Jumblies, but are not really likely to mention them outside a discussion of his verse. As for the runcible spoon, no one knows what it was like; it was Lear's little joke that we should not (and he makes it more difficult by having a runcible cat in another poem), just as Carroll gives us no help with frumious or vorpal.

Other children's writers have played the same game and modern science fiction is full of invented words. But will anyone ever remember them outside the limits of their own short-lived worlds? Of all fictional forms, adventures in Outer Space, especially on television, are the most ephemeral and the jargon invented to excite the children one year is forgotten by the next, having no literary merit to sustain it, as the Jabberwock and the Jumblies have. But even so, is a purely fictional life enough for a real word?

The question arises, what is a word? The dictionary says in essence that it is a sound or combination of sounds conveying, or helping to convey, an idea. By this standard some of the verbal inventions given above must fail to qualify. But a lot of nonsensical-sounding words that seem to come from nowhere do convey meanings to their hearers. Whoever first said he was flummoxed made his feelings clear, and so does anyone who complains of having been bamboozled or of feeling wonky, or who calls someone a nincompoop or a goop, or tells him to scram.

It may be objected that these last examples are only slang; but slang is the liveliest and most creative part of the language. The primitive people who provided most of our root-words had no standards of correctness; they spoke as the sounds came to them; and it is among those who most nearly resemble them, the least educated, the nearest to nature, that we may look for original creations. They will survive or not according to their merit. If expressive enough they will be repeated and may hang about in the jargon of some illiterate group for years, or centuries, before emerging to fill a gap in polite conversation.

I am always intrigued by the words in the Dictionary for which the editors, in spite of all their knowledge, can offer no origin. One of them is job which first appears as a low-class word for a menial task in the sixteenth century and has been slowly climbing the social ladder ever since. But what did it spring from? It has first been noted in some parish accounts of 1560 for a church in the Midlands where a man was paid threepence for 'fetching a jobbe of thorns' and again 'for three jobbes of straw'. It seems to have meant a pile or a load—perhaps a very local word—but the sense was soon transferred to the trouble of fetching it. In the next century, it had spread, with the sense of a small piece of work which was either insignificant or disreputable, and it flourished in thieves' cant. Now one can have a job in the Cabinet and no task is too great for this once humble word. Its use is also widening all the time. 'That's just the job,' we say, meaning the very thing we need.

Job is an example of a word for which no origin is known but that doesn't prove that it was a fresh creation in the sixteenth century. It may have begun then or earlier as no more than a scornful or comical sound that someone made to indicate an unimportant heap of something, perhaps a cross between a jot and a blob—I nearly wrote dob, but on looking it up find it is not given in the OED, and yet we do speak of a dob of paint—or at least I do. It only shows how easy it is to invent little words of this kind, and the whole story of job as far as we can see it illustrates the point that any kind of sound once attached to a mental concept, even in the most casual way, may grow into an acceptable word that can go on developing infinitely.

In modern times many of the new words that seem to spring up from nowhere to fill each gap as it occurs have developed in America. There is certainly a lively fount of creation there,

15

due partly to the mixed racial background, for half-remembered fragments of many old languages besides English are there for the picking up and may be passed around in merry back-chat among the semi-literate until their antecedents are quite lost. If they prove useful they will be adopted into more formal speech, and so spread round the world. Gimmick is one of these, bogus another, neither of any known origin. But most of the fresh creations from the States are at least partly derived from something we can recognise. Bulldozer obviously owes a great deal to the strength of the bull; and hijack, which seemed to leap forward the moment it was wanted and is now in the space of a few years unfortunately known to the whole world, seems to have come from truck drivers' slang, based on the simple shout of 'Hi Jack' when somebody hitched a lift and afterwards played a mean trick.

Some creation of words from almost nothing must still go on but generally it has some basis, however slight, on which to build. It comes most readily where there is a sense of humour and few academic inhibitions, and often the old trick of rhyming is brought into play to make a more telling effect. Hurly-burly, helter-skelter, hugger-mugger and flibberty-gibbet are all to be found in Shakespeare's plays or earlier, but we still play the same game. Recent coinages are razzmatazz, which is said to be a variation of razzle-dazzle, and fuddy-duddy, which has taken the place of old fogey (and fogey itself was unexplained). Now we are getting down to the nitty-gritty.

III

NEW WORDS FOR OLD

1 Compounds

Once any group of humans had some words—even a few—they could make more, for words beget words and multiply as people do. We can see them doing it during the whole period in which our language is on record, and we can assume that it always happened in much the same sort of way.

One of the commonest ways of making new words from old ones is the simple device of putting two together. The result is often a word that develops a strong character of its own, so individual that its separate parts may be quite forgotten. There are thousands of them and we never cease from making them: rainbow, sunrise, whirlpool, forehead, eyebrows, tiptoe, hedgehog, headstrong, seaside, postman, passport, football, are just a few that come to mind, each made up of two very obvious ingredients. There are as many more where either the spelling or the pronunciation, or both, have been contracted in the course of time—shepherd, holiday, breakfast, cupboard, for instance—but still the original words can be easily identified.

With many others of older vintage the two words have merged together so completely that they are no longer apparent as individuals. For example, alone is made of 'all one'. The solitary state of being one is intensified by 'all', so much so that when we have the two together as 'alone' we are still inclined to add 'all' again, crying with the ancient mariner '—all, all alone'. Once English speakers were accustomed to 'alone' they began sometimes to drop the a-, thus making 'lone', and from that came 'lonely', another word that poets have made much of, and then of course, loneliness and lonesome and so on.

Another example of a familiar word that is made up of two is answer. The second part of it is swear (OE *swarian*), not by using bad language but by making a solemn statement. As far back as our history goes, tribal leaders had to settle disputes and mete out justice of a sort to their people, and some of the earliest fragments of written English that exist are the laws of an eighth-century West Saxon king. One man would swear that another had wronged him and the accused man would also swear in reply. The exact words used were 'and swear', which became answer. That is why it still has a 'w' in it.

Going further back still, there are those two dignified old words, lord and lady, which seem as if they must always have been each a single entity. But although we see them in the eighth century already as single words, yet their earliest spellings betray their compound origins. The essential part of each of them is the loaf of bread, the making of which was a vital part of primitive man's achievements. The head of a household or a tribal group was the loaf-protector (early OE *hlaf weard*, later *hlaford*), and his wife was the loaf-kneader (*hlafdige*). By King Alfred's day these words were used as titles of respect for persons of rank, including the king and queen, and the connection with bread was probably quite forgotten, though there to be seen in the written word, rather as we can see the origin of cupboard but seldom think of cups on a shelf when we stow our various belongings into the modern piece of furniture.

The Anglo-Saxons were much inclined to create new words by adding prepositions in front of their verbs and nouns, and this produced hundreds of useful new words such as inside, outside, outcast, outlaw, overcome, overflow, offspring, foresee, downfall, uphold, overthrow, forestall, undergo, undertake, and so on. Prepositions are the main joints and sinews of the language, relating the more prominent words together, and used in this way they can help to create new words from old ones indefinitely.

In our day we are preposition mad, but mostly we add them after verbs as separate words instead of sticking them on in front. Sometimes they have no effect at all, as when we say 'meet up with' instead of just 'meet', but often they change the meaning entirely. To be put up is very different from being put up with, or put out, or put off, and one could go on endlessly with more examples. In this way we make new phrases at will to act as nouns or verbs such as dropout or sit-in, a habit that is very much in the English tradition, practised wherever English is spoken, and unabated after a thousand years. Indeed, the Americans are almost more addicted to it than we are, adding prepositions fore and aft, attached or unattached with great abandon. When they say 'for free' and 'for real', nothing is added to the meanings of free and real, but 'uptight' says something new, and in pure Anglo-Saxon style.

Coinages of this sort are highly idiomatic and liable to change, especially those in which the prepositions remain separate. Which will last for posterity and which disappear the quickest no one can tell, but the law of the survival of the fittest operates very strongly in the field of language.

Turning back to the older words that have endured so well, we may be sometimes puzzled—if we stop to think of it which few do—as to how the separate parts add up to the final meaning. Take 'understand', for example, which had just the same meaning for the Anglo-Saxons as it has for us. It must, I think, have arisen from the idea of a leader having men under him. To 'stand under' a man might well have signified that you were his loyal follower, perhaps in his confidence, so that you felt you knew his mind. In some such way the sense we know may have come about.

The familiar preposition 'with' had a different meaning in the remote past from the one we know. It expressed a feeling of opposition which is the very reverse of its later sense, and this old meaning is still in use when we say that a man fights with his enemies, quarrels with his neighbours, or argues with his wife. But the antagonism was always close at hand and reciprocated, so that gradually this sense of nearness and a joint activity prevailed over the opposedness, giving way to togetherness. However, the early meaning survives in withhold, withdraw and withstand.

Compound words are of several sorts. Those mentioned first in this section, such as rainbow and whirlpool, are true partnerships, each of two words of equal interest. In those that are formed with prepositions, the other part is the more important. We might pass on to the addition of mere prefixes and suffixes—verbal fragments used only for word-building—but those that have never been independent words in their own right can be set aside for the moment. However, there are some that have had separate lives of their own and yet have been added so regularly to others that in that respect they are thought of as suffixes and have acquired a shortened form.

I am thinking of words like full. Careful means full of care, and full is as good a word as care, but we use it in this way so often—joyful, thankful and all the rest of them—that we give it only one 'l' in this position as if to stress its subordinate state. We may then add a true suffix and make carefulness; -ness has never been an independent word (it has nothing to do with the geographical feature), and its only function in our language is to turn adjectives into abstract nouns which it has been doing consistently ever since our records begin.

Another old suffix for forming abstract nouns and one which, unlike -ness, has been an important word on its own account is -dom. In Old English dōm meant judgement. We see it in this sense in doomsday, and still use it as doom, a word that has grown more and more gloomy over the years. Prophets of doom predict only the worst. There was nothing of this in its early meaning. Kingdom was a compound of two equal parts, the jurisdiction of a king with nothing bad about it, so also earldom, dukedom and the rest. But in this secondary position -dom became vaguer and wider in meaning. In freedom and wisdom it signifies only the state of being (free or wise). In fact it became a suffix. We don't use it a great deal now, though an actor can rise to stardom, and in the modern words officialdom and (even better) bumbledom the old sense of ruling is in use again, and in a way that we don't like. Meanwhile as a separate word the old doom has lost nothing of its force.

It is rather the same with the ending -ship, which has nothing to do with sea-going craft. It is an offshoot of the verb to shape, which in Old English as *scieppan* (the sound 'sh' was then written 'sc') meant to create. In one of the oldest surviving fragments of English poetry, Caedmon's lines on the Creation, God is the 'holy Shaper' of the earth. The ordinary word, shape, is still as strong as ever, but when it was added to other nouns its vowel became shortened through being unstressed (as with doom and -dom) and its sense more abstract, implying not physical shape but a general state or condition as in township, friendship, and so forth. The Anglo-Saxons used also to talk of beership (*ge-beorscype*), meaning the conviviality of a drinking party, but that useful expression has gone.

As a suffix, -ship is still active, especially for forming abstract nouns from official titles. We add it to any of them however long, happily making vicechairmanship, undersecretaryship and the like. Thus from compound words we progress to complex ones, too complex sometimes. But a recent example that can hardly be faulted is oneupmanship. Made of four Old English words, it neatly expresses in one word a concept that formerly required a whole phrase, naming a human foible that can often call for comment.

In general, compound words have more precise meanings than the sum of their separate parts. A waterfall is not just falling water—not rain, for instance, or water falling from a tap. It is exactly the natural feature for which the word was created. Again, an upstart isn't *anyone* who starts up. It carries a strong implication that he should not have started up and should be put down again. It was obviously first spoken in anger and a feeling of annoyance still clings about it. That is an intriguing thought about words, especially compound ones; they were all coined once for the first time, tailormade for a special occasion, and only if they fulfilled that purpose well were they remembered and repeated by others.

The second universal law in language—besides survival of the fittest, just mentioned—is that of supply and demand. A successful word is created because it is wanted, and for immediate use. A cabinet-maker might devise and make a new piece of furniture hoping someone would buy it as a novelty, but nobody ever coined a lasting word except to express his thoughts or feelings, or to give information on a subject for which he could find no adequate existing word. And as most of our language was created verbally, the new word was put instantly to the test, its success depending on the comprehension of the hearer. If the message was received as intended, it was fairly launched.

2 Grammar and Words

It is not my purpose to dwell on questions of grammar beyond the barest minimum, but when we look for the different ways in which new words have been made out of old ones, we find at once that a vast number have come into being as the direct result of varying grammatical forms, especially from very early times. You might expect primitive languages to have the simplest of grammar, but this is not so. Not that primitive people ever thought about grammar or consciously devised abstract nouns, past participles or the like, but they did want to communicate more and more effectively with their companions and in their efforts to express more exact shades of meaning were constantly making minor additions or changes to their words to modify the sense. So grammatical systems developed willy-nilly, and complications grew. But then in time the pendulum could swing the other way and more sophisticated people could prune away some of the excrescences of their speech habits, so that the later language may be simpler than the earlier. This certainly happened to English.

Anyone who has learnt Greek (ancient or modern), Latin, Russian or German, knows what grammatical complications can be. Old English had them all, case inflexions, unnatural genders, adjectives that must agree with nouns, the lot. But in the period after the Conquest when the literate, such as they were, wrote in Latin or Norman French, and English existed only as a spoken language, it shook off most of these encumbrances with extraordinary vigour, finding itself other ways of attaining clarity.

To me, one of the greatest mysteries of language is the concept inherited by all the Indo-European languages of all words being divided into two or three groups, known as genders, but not related—or not consistently—to anything in nature. To English people, accustomed to a language

23

that has freed itself from this strange tyranny, it is the hardest part of learning a foreign language and only to be mastered by long practice. To the rest of Europe the genders of their own vocabularies come almost by instinct. Even young children and illiterate people who speak badly in general are never at fault in this respect, and when the floundering Englishman in France refers to a table as 'he' instead of 'she', it grates on the French hearer more painfully than any other kind of error.

As for the agreement of adjectives with nouns—English is the only language in Europe in which you can speak of a tall man, a tall woman, a tall tree and tall people without any change in the qualifying word; the only one where the article is never varied. In German 'the' has six different forms and in modern Greek twelve, and then you must know which one to use in sixteen or eighteen different combinations of case, gender and number.

The great simplification of English grammar took place gradually during the Middle Ages and it must often have seemed to the older people who remembered how their fathers and grandfathers had spoken that their language was in a state of total decay. To hear people saying 'handes' instead of the old *handa* sounded as wrong to them as when we hear a child say 'foots' for feet. One doesn't mind it in a child because he will learn, but in the thirteenth century or thereabouts the old grammatical forms were forgotten on every side. But out of chaos a simpler and better order was evolved.

There were two main trends. One was the dropping of all unnecessary inflexions—and few are really needed for understanding. From adjectives all were dropped and from nouns nearly all. This was achieved without loss of clarity by observing a logical order of words and a plentiful use of prepositions. When we say that the dog bit the cat, there is no need to alter the word cat to stress what has happened provided it follows the verb; and if you go to town, there is no need to add a syllable to 'town', for 'to' has already made all clear. But the Anglo-Saxons did both these things. The other trend was towards consistency. For nouns the only case-endings that were preserved were those that indicated the plural and the state of possession; and instead of having five or six different endings for each of them, as there had been earlier, one standard form for each (with some slight spelling variation) became the normal practice. Of course it wasn't all done at once or on any plan; it just happened in colloquial speech, and rather unluckily it chanced that the endings that survived for these two separate functions were almost identical in form. For plurals one of the Old English inflexions had been -as and this, modified to -es or -s, was almost universally adopted. (We might just as well have had -en, another very common old plural.) For genitives there was again a choice of several but -es was the one preferred. We now make this look different from the plural ending by writing it 's, but this is no help with the spoken word.

The English seem to have a strange predilection for ending words with -s, for this letter has also provided one of our few modern inflexions for verbs. The older ending for the third person singular was -eth (he giveth) and this lasted just long enough to be used by Shakespeare occasionally and in the King James's Bible, but by then it was old-fashioned and losing ground rapidly to the popular -s.

This tendency to use a final -s as the maid-of-all-work of English grammar, combined with the dropping of so many of the old inflexions that had distinguished one part of speech from another, has led to easy fluent speech, but it has its drawbacks too. It can be ambiguous at times, especially in brief phrases like newspaper headings. 'Police claim mounts.' Both claim and mounts can be verb or noun. Police can be noun or adjective. Do they want horses or is their claim growing? We can guess, but this sort of thing can come hard on foreigners.

Returning briefly to the plurals of nouns, we should note

25

that only the merest handful of Old English ones were strong enough to stand firm against the epidemic of 's' endings. Those that did are amongst our oldest and most basic words, so familiar in use that nothing could change them. Taken as a group they give a homely picture of the medieval household—men, women, children, teeth, feet, oxen, geese, mice and lice. Brethren hung on for a bit, but is barely alive. Shoon and eyen (or eyne) lasted to Chaucer's time but barely to Shakespeare's, and that is really all, except for the very few, like sheep and deer, which have never made any change in the plural.

The salient feature of most of this small band is that they become plural by changing their central vowel. At an early stage in the development of the language, internal vowels were very apt to change from various causes, and not only in nouns for a great number of our oldest and commonest verbs showed the differences of tenses in this way. Many of them still do—run/ran, give/gave, take/took, fly/flew, come/came, ride/rode, and so on—but in Old English there were far more of this type. If some of them had not lost their old 'strong' forms and joined the ranks of those that make their past tenses by adding -ed (and are called 'weak'), we should still be saying 'I holp' instead of 'I helped'.

We come back to the point that words beget words and the more their original forms varied the more diversified are their offshoots. In English there are dozens of pairs of words directly derived from each other long ago but seeming quite separate because of the change of vowel. A road is where you ride, a knot is what you knit, and a flood has flowed. You strew the straw, sing a song, sit on a seat, feed on food, scrape a scrap and skim the scum. Then you can sow the seed, mow the mead, throw a thread (in spinning)—and so we might go on.

In Old English the ending -th was regularly used for making abstract nouns from verbs. Any addition to them was likely to affect the original vowel and in these -th words it often changes, though not always. From steal we have stealth, from grow growth, from brew broth, from gird girth, and of course you gird your girth with a girdle. From the verb to bear comes birth, and from die, death (by way of dead which itself comes from the past tense). From rue comes ruth, which we hardly ever use now except as a girl's name or in the negative form ruthless, which is useful for describing tyrants. And from the verb to mow came an old noun, *math*, so that when the mowing was done you were left with the aftermath.

'Th' can be added to nouns too (from moon, for example, comes month), but most of all it goes with adjectives. We are all familiar with such pairs as wide/width, strong/strength and true/truth, but perhaps some of the following are less obvious: merry/mirth, slow/sloth, foul/filth, young/youth, hale/health, well/wealth, dry/drought (earlier, drouth) and dear/dearth. The last one may seem surprising, but the oldest meaning we know of dear was precious, highly valued, and hence rare and in short supply (as well as greatly loved).

The suffix -th has had its day and is no longer used for new coinages except jokingly. Coolth, first noted in the sixteenth century, and greenth, in the eighteenth, have indeed found places in the dictionary but they remain oddities. I like coolth and feel I could use it on summer evenings, especially since coolness has become so personal. Of all the Old English noun suffixes, the one with the most life in it—undiminished life— is -ness, and we happily add this to any adjective, however modern. I noted poshness on the radio the other day. I don't say that I care for it, but it shows the vitality of -ness.

We have always had a great choice of prefixes and suffixes, both from Old English and abroad, and with them can build a dozen or more words from one root. Take, for instance, hale from the list above. It is the northern form of whole, meaning complete, perfect, well. So, to start with, the word has two separate forms. From whole we have wholly, whole-some, unwholesome, wholesomeness and several more.

27

From hale comes the verb to heal, and from that come healer and healing, and the latter can be an independent noun or an adjective as well as part of the verb. Then we have health, healthy, healthily, healthful, unhealthy, unhealthiness and so on. And there is also the verb to hail, which seems entirely different but comes from wishing a friend 'Health' and calling it out as a greeting.

But that is not all. The basic root *hāl-* gave rise also to holy (for an OE long *ā* generally turned to a long 'o' in southern England). The meaning is much the same for whereas hale refers to physical perfection, holy means perfect in the spiritual sense. From holy came holiness, unholy, and a few more. There was also the verb to hallow, to make holy or treat as holy, and this was formerly used, too, as a noun for a holy person whom we now call a saint: but this is almost obsolete except in such phrases as All Hallows Church or Halloween. Here then are twenty words and more, all formed with various affixes from the one root *hāl-*. Truly words grow from words.

3   New Meanings

New words can be made endlessly by adding more material to existing ones, but old words can also be used again without any change in such different ways that they seem like original creations. You may say that a word used in a changed sense is not a new word. Perhaps not, but it serves the purpose.

Think of 'bow' which has developed senses so distinct that one of them has even acquired a different pronunciation. To start with we have the Old English *bogan*, to bend, from which came the noun meaning a bent or curved thing, like the hunter's bow or a rainbow. Much later a piece of string or ribbon that was bent or looped around in a special way was said to be tied in a bow. Meanwhile a man could bow himself into a human curve, and in this case the vowel was somewhat changed. There are other meanings too, but that is enough to make the point; we may in fact be using one word for the hunter's weapon, the courtier's gesture and the bow we tie, but we think of them as three.

Again, think of 'spring' which started out as OE *springan*, to leap up, and continues in the same sense. All Old English verbs ended in *-an* or *-ian*, an inflexion which most of them lost (though it occasionally survives as -en, as in sharpen), and once the inflexion was gone, spring could be a noun or a verb. So it could serve for the bubbling or leaping up of water out of the ground, or the growing up of vegetation after the winter, and in more modern times when resilient metal coils were devised to give a mechanical upward push, the same word served again. The natural leap, the place to fill your bucket, the growing season and the metal coil—the word we use for them all seems like four.

Or consider the watch kept on ships, a period of time; or the watch kept by guards anywhere, an abstract noun for their careful action, though it could also be applied to the guards themselves. And then consider the watch on your wrist, a material object that seems completely different from those others. But the word for them all is the same, derived from the Old English *wæccian*, to wake or stay awake. It was not till the sixteenth century that it was applied to a portable timepiece such as might be used when keeping watch. Before that any mechanical timekeeper was called a clock, so named from the sound of its striking bell.

There has always been a tendency to call man-made objects by the name of the substance of which they are made, even long after they have ceased to be made that way. We talk of doing the ironing though the piece of electrical equipment we use contains no iron; and when we use a household broom we give no thought to the wild broom that still grows on our hillsides or is maybe cultivated in our gardens. In earlier times housewives would bind together bunches of its twigs to sweep their houses; so came the name for the household article now far removed from nature.

The plant whose product has made the biggest contribution to the language is undoubtedly flax, of which linen is made. 'Flax' is a Germanic word that the Anglo-Saxons used for the plant, but they also at an early date knew the Latin word *linum* and they called the fibrous thread that the plant yielded by their own version of it (*lín*) and the cloth they wove of it was linen. Line, to give it its modern spelling, has produced a wealth of meanings: first any kind of string or cord, such as a fishing-line or a clothes-line, then anything running in a continuous direction, like lines of printed letters or metal lines for trains to run on. Then, stretching wider and wider, the routes on which ships travel—hence liners—and the whole organisation behind them; and now following from that we have airlines and air liners. And again there are metaphorical uses, still implying general direction—a line of conduct, or a line of business, or of argument, or of ancestry. And all these lines have further ramifications of their own.

So much for the noun. As a verb, line took a different course, more closely related to the fabric. A rough woollen garment was the better for having a layer of smoother stuff inside it and this in the early Middle Ages was normally made of linen. So to line something was to put linen underneath it. But this meaning was soon extended to anything that went inside, and you could have a lining of silk or fur, or 'a fair round belly with good capon lined'.

These examples are just a selection of the widely differing concepts we express by means of the natural fibre of the flax plant. They have brought us into the world of metaphor and show how easy it is to slip from a natural extension of the literal meaning to one that is purely figurative. When the word for a linen thread is stretched out to an imaginary line that goes right round the world, the dictionary can still call this an 'extended meaning', but when we reach something as abstract as a line of discussion, it has become a metaphor. We use a similar idea when we speak of the thread of the argument.

Most of the oldest common nouns have metaphorical uses, and the abstract nouns with which we habitually express our thoughts can generally be traced back to simple material objects. Way used to mean the track, path or road in the physical sense, and we keep this meaning of the actual surface in compounds such as roadway, runway, and motorway, but when we ask the way to a place we are thinking more of the general direction and means of transport, and far more often the use is completely abstract, signifying method or style: the way he talks—the way they behave—the way she does her hair.

Almost every part of the body can be used metaphorically, some for abstract qualities, some for other physical objects as, for instance, features of the landscape: a headland or (Beachey) Head, the foot of the cliff, the mouth of the river, the brow of the hill, an arm of the sea, a neck of land. And because it was formerly believed that the heart was the centre not only of life but of thought and feeling too, so heart has made a particularly large contribution to our vocabulary. Although we have known for some time that our emotions

31

are centred in our brain, we go on regardless of this describing someone as brokenhearted, lighthearted, having lost his heart or won his heart's desire. The mental and emotional states implied by this word are very various and far from logical. To be heartless might mean only to lack feeling, but it is worse than that, positively cruel. In contrast one might expect hearty to mean kind and loving. But no, it refers to physical energy; one can even eat a hearty breakfast, and too much heartiness can become tiresome. To hearten is to put new life in someone, while disheartening news weakens his spirit.

Then think of hand; not so vital a part as the heart, but the one that has enabled us to make things and master our environment. No wonder the hand has made many words. First comes the literal meaning, then figuratively 'Give me a hand' (help), or theatrically 'Give him a good hand' (applause), or a hand at cards, or factory hands. Or as a verb, 'Hand me the book', or with various prepositions, hand out, hand over and others. Then again a secondary verb, handle, and in exactly the same form the useful noun for the material object made to be gripped by the hand. To be handy is to be good with your hands or convenient to the hand—a handy tool. Or it may signify being near 'at hand', that is, within easy reach, and this can be extended further so that you can describe a house as handy for the bus stop, and the bus as handy for the shops. A handful has at least two meanings: 'Only a handful of people came' (very few) or 'That boy is a handful' (too much to manage easily). But of all the derivatives of hand, the one that has wandered farthest from the basic meaning is handsome. It springs from the idea of giving. One who hands out freely is generous, and such a person is admired and noble, and may be so in appearance. The idea of generosity is expressed in the phrase 'A handsome sum was collected'. It implies something large and the good looks are also on a large scale—a better word for men than women, and for public buildings than for cottages.

What with the many meanings, literal and figurative, and the changes made by prefixes and suffixes—not to mention compounds such as handicraft and handicap (which originated as a game of chance in which tokens of good or bad luck were drawn from a cap), the hand has probably provided more words than any other part of the body, but the heart runs it close.

Our speech is so riddled with metaphors we can hardly say a sentence without one. Politicians are particularly fond of them and I am not thinking of the well-worn phrases about putting shoulders to the wheel and exploring avenues, but of the single words which they ceaselessly find to deal with new situations. They discuss putting a ceiling on prices or freezing or pegging them, sometimes both in one sentence, while others seek to escape from the straitjacket of restraint or complain of kangaroo courts and wild-cat strikes. Such vivid expressions attract our attention but the language is also full of older-established metaphors that pass unheeded: the root of the matter, the hub of industry, the drain on resources, a storm of protest, a barrage of questions, a torrent of abuse, the rising tide of unemployment, muck-raking, slush money—how wet a lot of it sounds. Even the most ordinary phrases, like the handling of the affair or the course of events, are metaphors. The basic meaning of 'course' was running or galloping—later, the place where one did it. A career, on the other hand, was entirely on horseback, specifically the charge of a knight in the lists, short and violent. Now it tends to be long and slow. It may rise to a peak, or be chequered or blighted, or even end in shipwreck.

There is nothing new in this sort of talk. As far back as we can see, our remote forefathers having got a word for one thing did not hesitate to use it for another provided there was some linking idea however farfetched. Many of our commonest words echo their fancies. A window started as the wind's eye in the days when the wind looked in with a chilly glance through unglazed apertures. A daisy is the

33

day's eye. Wildflower names are largely metaphorical, and I always think that foxgloves must have been first made up by a child. Children have always loved fitting the trumpet-shaped blooms on their fingers (Roman children, too, judging by the Latin *digitalis*), but the notion of putting them on a fox is an absurdity of our own. Some say, in an attempt to explain it, that this name is a corruption of folk's glove. But as early as the year 1,000 it appears in a Saxon herbal as *foxes glofa* and at that date 'folk's' would have been *folces* with the 'l' clearly sounded.

But metaphors are not all pretty by any means. The language of abuse depends very largely on them and always has. It would be easy to make a list of extremely unpleasant metaphors if one wanted to, which I don't.

In fact the same words can be put to endless different uses and are seldom the worse for it. Sometimes a word is spoilt by stupid or excessive use, but most of them go on and on, their vitality undiminished by centuries of hard wear.

4 Ramifications

Yet another way in which words proliferate is through the tendency of language to split into different dialects so that two forms of the same word may exist side by side. Who would think that daft and deft could ever have been the same word? In Old English *dæfte* meant gentle or docile. In the south, as deft, it came to be good with one's hands. But in the more rugged north to be mild and gentle was thought silly, and there the word was pronounced daft.

Many pairs of words have split in this sort of way. Skirt and shirt, for example, are the same in origin. The 'sk' sound in Danish had a softer 'sh' sound in Anglo-Saxon, and in about the tenth century this word in either form referred to the loose linen garment worn under the tunic by Danes and Saxons alike. The variation of meaning by which northerners came to apply the word to the lower part of the garment as skirt, and southerners to the upper part as shirt, is pure chance. Now all English speakers have both words.

But dialect variations can give far more than two words from one, especially when words have been divided from each other long ago. How would we have such a number of similar words for shining in the dark as glow, gleam, glimmer, glint, glitter, glister and glisten, if they had not all grown from the same root but been shaped and modified variously by different communities of speakers, and then eventually come together in the standard language?

This gl- theme can be carried further, for glimpse is related to glimmer in its early meaning of a quick flash of light. The first known meaning of glad is bright, and a glade is a bright part of a forest where sunlight falls because the trees are less dense. If we could see far enough back we could perhaps connect glass, glaze, gloss and glare, and link up with the Latin *gloria*. Somewhere far behind all these must be the light of prehistoric fires glowing in the darkness and a spoken sound associated with them that ramified across Europe, reaching

England in several forms that have diversified further. Sometimes the meaning concentrates on the light, sometimes on the semi-darkness as in the Scottish gloaming, but there are far too many of them for the resemblance to be chance.

In ancient pre-literate times in north-eastern Europe somewhere between the Baltic and the Black Sea, or so the scholars tell us, the language that they call Indo-European split into its main branches as its speakers wandered off in different directions, some south-eastwards into Asia, some westwards across Europe. These principal branches—Indo-Iranian, Armenian, Greek, Latin, Slavonic, Celtic and Germanic—are now so different that they seem like separate growths, and yet many of their most basic words have sprung from the same ancient roots.

The oldest examples of Indo-European literature in any considerable quantity are the Hindu Vedas, written in Sanscrit, the parent of Hindi, Persian and other west-Asian languages. In these sacred books, some of which date from before 1000 BC, scholars can get their first view of some words that are still current in Europe, and see the links between our widely differing languages. To take only one example, the English word 'night' may be linked with the Sanscrit *nacta* and compared with modern Greek *nichta*, Italian *notte*, Russian *noch*, Welsh *nos* and German *nacht*.

As the main branches of this great Indo-European language spread further and further apart over thousands of miles they all kept on dividing and subdividing, and the one that concerns us, Germanic, eventually provided languages for all the territory known as Germany (which has been linked more by language than political union), for several of its neighbours, including Holland, for all the Scandinavian countries, and for England; and at the time when the tribes of Angles and Saxons were invading Britain, all these Germanic tongues were nearer together than they are now. It follows that when about three centuries later another wave of invaders, this time from Denmark and Norway, came also to seize a share of Britain, their language was closely akin to that of the Angles among whom they settled. For a time it was spoken as a separate language in parts of the north, but eventually merged with English, its chief effect being to accentuate the dialect difference between north and south.

The word dialect to the modern ear generally signifies a survival of local speech from the past which is considered quaint, amusing, attractive, but not correct because it differs from the standard form. But another equally valid meaning is that of different branches of the same language of which none is necessarily better than another. In this sense the Anglo-Saxons spoke in several dialects of which the most important were Anglian in the north and the Midlands, West Saxon in the greater part of the south, and Kentish in the south-east. Each of these, especially Anglian, had several subdivisions. It was not until the fifteenth century that the language of London and the universities, which was chiefly East Midland in character, emerged as the standard to which the others gradually conformed.

But not all the regions have conformed entirely. The northern counties are still markedly different in speech from the south, and the English of Scotland, another direct descendant of early Anglian, retains its distinctive pronunciation and much of its own vocabulary, and that without any loss of respect from others. Moreover, this Scottish English has not only kept its own character, though somewhat modified and more like southern English than it used to be, but has carried it all over the world and may be instantly recognised and enjoyed—for it is charming to the ear—from Canada to New Zealand.

On the whole, the different dialects of England have either faded away or grown back into the main trunk increasing its strength. The metaphor of a tree breaks down here for real branches do not behave like that. Linguistic branches do strange things not found in nature; they can grow quite different from each other as they move apart and some of them can grow to inordinate lengths. Look what our own branch has done. A thousand years ago it was spoken by less than a million people in one small island. Now it has sent out enormous new branches across the world, each with creative powers of its own. American English is one; Canadian, being so close to it, is very similar in character; Australian, far from these two, is already quite distinctive; and each remote region where English is spoken has its own specialities.

But though all these vigorous young branches have deviated to some extent from the main trunk—which itself continues to grow and change—they have done so only in details, because the easy communications of modern times, the common literary heritage, the enjoyment of the same entertainment and anxiety about the same problems hold them together. The outward pull of spontaneous growth is as strong as ever it was, but the modern bonds are strong too.

Even our antiquated spelling, which it seems so impossible to change except minimally, acts as a restraint. The Americans have modified it slightly but not enough to have much effect. Where pronunciation varies from one country to another, the words still look alike. The American talks of his 'ant' and the Englishman of his 'ahnt' but both have the same mental picture of 'aunt' and that is what they write in their letters.

Since English has become a world language it now has other branches growing among people who have no physical Anglo-Saxon inheritance. In India it is the chief official language though not the native tongue of those who speak it. Inevitably they must develop their own style of pronunciation and their special idioms; and the same is happening in many African countries whose native tongues are totally alien to English and yet who use it to communicate with each other and with the rest of the world. Again there are influences to prevent too much change. Trade, diplomacy and air travel (which is conducted in English all round the globe), radio, television and films from England and America, all help to hold the vast growth together; and yet language is never static and such varied conditions must bring change.

In lands where English is learned as a second language, it has a formality that may keep it stable for a time, but where it is the first and natural tongue of most of the people there is a constant fluidity and creativity that nothing can check, new meanings for old words, new constructions out of old material; and as any of these can easily pass, if wanted, from one land to another, the total result is more words for all of us—and I am not now thinking of borrowings from other languages, only of variations of our own old stock.

Sometimes a dialect word that is nearly forgotten in England can be revived overseas to a new life. The Old English verb, to go, had a northern form *gangan* which lingered long in Scotland and the north of England after it had disappeared from the south. We meet it often in Burns's poems. 'The best laid schemes of mice and men gang aft agley.' In modern English it survives in 'gangway' but it was also used for a group of itinerant workmen who used to gang or go together, such as the gangs of navvies who dug the canals and laid the first railways. This usage was carried to America, where it took a more sinister turn. Gang became a menacing word, and from it came gangster, a coinage that has spread quickly round the world.

Or there is the noun, rig, which we use now for the amazing contraptions that can stand in the North Sea. The name comes direct from Texas where the first oil rigs were set up in the nineteenth century. But at least five hundred years before that, rig was a common word in nautical speech around the coasts of Britain. To rig was to fix up, generally with the aid of ropes, hence rigging on ships. In England it had many colloquial uses, including an outfit of clothes, long before the Texans rigged up their apparatus for extracting oil, and gave it the meaning that has now become so important in British politics.

And then for something very different there is that happy compound, walkabout, now much in vogue in England in a specific new significance, though nothing could be less like the Aborigines' habit of wandering off into the Bush (for which the Australians coined it) than the new royal style of mingling with large crowds. It was in New Zealand that it was first applied in this way, when the Queen, breaking with tradition, walked freely among the people in the streets of Wellington. They all had to talk of it and the Australian word came to their lips. Jubilee Year brought walkabouts to Britain, and politicians have taken up the same expression too.

So the same words go round and round, and the old stock with its roots too deep to be ever unearthed renews itself from one branch to another, in a way which would in a real tree be most peculiar. But what will happen to these branches next? Will they grow more and more separate and different, or become more mutually entangled? No one knows the answer any more than we know the fate of the civilized world. It may be in another century or two that a kind of formal, traditional English will be used all round the world for international affairs as Latin was in medieval Europe, while each of the old English-speaking lands develops its own vernacular. We just don't know.

5 Places and People

Yet another way of making new words out of well-worn material—a roundabout method, but one that has produced some familiar words—is by making use of proper nouns.

The names of places and persons, though often formed originally from ordinary words, have yet acquired a special individual character that keeps them separate and apart. However, in some circumstances they can return again into general circulation in a new use.

The most usual way for this to happen is when an article or commodity is called after its inventor, such as mackintosh, a kind of rubberised cloth patented by Charles Mackintosh in 1843. For over a century his name was supreme in this department, often shortened to mack, but now that so many other waterproof materials are available we are more inclined to talk of raincoats.

Or maybe it is a manufacturer's name that passes into the language, like that of the Hoover Company, which is only one of several well-known makers of vacuum cleaners. In this case I am sure that the reason for this trade-name being such a favourite with English housewives (even when using a different make) is that it has such a suitable sound. 'I'm just hoovering the carpet,' is satisfying to the ear, almost onomatopoeic.

Or the name of a botanist may be given to a new plant that he has grown or introduced, such as dahlia from Mr Dahl of Sweden, magnolia from M. Magnol of France, and buddleia from the Reverend Mr Buddle, an Essex parson of Queen Anne's time, whose name sounds rather better as a shrub than as a surname.

Or garments may be known by the names of famous people who wore that sort of thing, like Wellington boots, common enough in England (unknown in America) to be written wellingtons (no word quite qualifies in this class unless it has lost its capital letter) or even wellies, which has now gained a place in the OED.

Another in the clothing category is cardigan, also named after a general, and this one makes a good example of how a word can pass from one class to another, changing its meaning at each step. The knitted jacket takes its name from the seventh Earl of Cardigan, the one who led the famous charge of the Light Brigade, the bitter cold of the Crimea being enough to account for extra warm garments. His title came from the old Welsh county of Cardigan, not that he was even partly Welsh, for Welsh place-names were often given as titles to the English nobility without any justifying link. The place took its name from a Celtic prince, Ceredigion ap Maelgwyn, a ruler of that region in the sixth century. So to reverse the order we have a personal name, a place-name, a title and a knitted jacket, the whole evolution covering thirteen hundred years.

Of the common nouns derived from personal idiosyncrasies the one that has had the most remarkable success in the world is undoubtedly sandwich. Once again we have an earl, this one of the eighteenth century, his title springing from the Kentish town of Sandwich (village in the sand in plain Old English). Though holding high office in government he was also a compulsive gambler and, being often unwilling to leave the card table to have his dinner, would call for slices of bread and beef and eat them while he played. It must have been in the clubs that he frequented that these snacks were first called jokingly by his name; then it spread around London and now round the world. Few other English words, if any, have been adopted into so many foreign languages and it may be supposed that there is never a minute when thousands of people, if not millions, are not uttering the word sandwich.

One more personal name that has proliferated in an extraordinary way is guy, as used in America for a man or by the young for either sex. It can only come from Guy Fawkes, but why a whole nation that doesn't keep Guy Fawkes Day and knows little about him should have taken up his name in such a way remains a mystery. In England the reason why his name and his day are so strongly remembered is not because of his failure to blow up Parliament—there are many far more important events in our history that go un-remembered—nor because of his horrible death which was a commonplace at that time; it is just that it happened to coin-cide with the old pagan autumnal festival of the dead, which the church had sanctified as All Saints Day, its eve being popularly celebrated as Halloween. The old urge to make bonfires at this time of year—with attendant fun and games—was switched to the burning of Guy, and his name passed into the language as a hideous effigy, and then more generally as a person who looks ridiculous, or a verb to mock. It must have been from these later developments that Americans first called each other guys in a joking spirit. But it is strange how the habit grew, while the critical sense was lost. Of course like all the most popular Americanisms it is also heard all over the world.

If Guy Fawkes can take no credit for what happened to his name, nor can Captain Boycott. Once again we must go back to a place-name, that of a small village in Shropshire where someone called Boi or Boia had his humble cot before the writing of Domesday Book. Like so many village names it was later used as the surname of a family who must have lived there once, and then we jump on to 1880 when a certain Captain Boycott was agent for the estates of an Irish earl in County Mayo. He was so unpopular with the tenants that labourers would not work for him, shop-keepers serve him, or innkeepers accommodate him and he eventually had to leave the country, little knowing that he had provided English and the world with a new verb.

This trick of turning personal names into ordinary parts of speech is not a regular process. There is often something odd and haphazard about it but that is like human nature and we may suppose that this sort of thing has always happened. The examples just given are ones where the origins are well-known, being mostly concerned with prominent men, but there must be other cases where the names of obscurer people of long ago have provided words for which we now know no roots.

The same thing has often happened among the French and their words in many cases come on to us. Think, for instance, of sadism from the cruel Marquis de Sade, also of guillotine and silhouette. Joseph Guillotin was a kindly doctor who wanted to make capital punishment quick and painless. In contrast Etienne de Silhouette was an unpopular politician whose name was given by his enemies to a new kind of fashionable portraiture to suggest that his plans were mere shadowy outlines with nothing in them. What was meant as an unkind jibe has given him immortality, for his name, being unusual and euphonious, has stuck to this kind of picture and passed to the wider meaning of any object seen against the light. It lives on in a pleasant, artistic atmosphere, while the name of the humane doctor is associated with severity and horror, and is none the better for its frequent metaphorical use in our parliament.

These things often work out most unfairly. Just think of the Goths and Vandals who ravaged the Roman empire in its years of decline. I suppose there was nothing to choose between them in their habits of violence and destruction. And yet 'Gothic' is chiefly associated with an inspired and inspiring style of architecture, developed long after the Goths had disappeared, and all the worst qualities of both tribes are loaded on the vandal.

Going still farther back, the classical gods and goddesses of Greece and Rome have been a source for word-making since ancient times, used in all the lands that have inherited their culture. Cereal from Ceres, volcano from Vulcan, jovial from Jove and erotic from Eros, are just a few examples, and modern scientists still dip into the same ancient source to produce such names as vulcanite and plutonium.

Place-names, too, can become ordinary words and we have china for the kind of porcelain that first came from China, then extended to much commoner crockery, currants from Corinth, port wine from Oporto, canaries from the Canary Islands (which literally in Spanish means Isle of Dogs), and turkeys *not* from Turkey. Those arising from popular error make just as good words as the ones that are based on fact. The name of Turkey was first applied to a bird when some guinea fowl were brought back from the west coast of Africa in Tudor times. The creatures were strange, outlandish, from some very foreign place—as it might be Turkey. And when the Pilgrim Fathers found some other strange birds—even bigger and better—in New England, they used this same word for them. It was just the same with gipsies. They came from—goodness knows where—somewhere beyond Europe, like for instance Egypt. That was remote enough. So they were Egyptians, soon shortened to gipsies, an original word coined out of ignorance and yet seeming to suit them, though they don't use it themselves.

So we can make a word to suit us out of almost anything but we must have a bit of material to start us off. When we say a place or a person or a happening is romantic, do we ever have in mind the least idea that it is Roman, or anything to do with Rome? But that is clearly the base of the word. Briefly, it comes from Romance, which after the break-up of the Roman Empire was the name used for the languages descended from Latin. Then it came to mean the stories told in those languages, tales of love and adventure that came into England from France and Italy in the Middle Ages. In France the word has remained literary, *romance* being still used chiefly for the language group, while *un roman* is a novel; but in England romance has taken off and flown into a world

45

of happy love that need not be fictitious. As for romantic, our use of it is not easy to define, but we know exactly what we mean by it, and have no other word that expresses that feeling quite so well.

IV

ADOPTIONS

1 Kinds of Borrowing

Words of foreign origin that have found their way into English are generally called borrowings or loan-words. These expressions seem to me unapt, for when one borrows something it is on the strict understanding that it will be returned, and who ever thought of returning a word to the French or Italians or anyone else from whom we had filched it? For one thing we haven't deprived them of it, and for another they might not want it after what we have done to it, for we are apt to treat our borrowings rather roughly.

However, the meanings of words are established not by logic but by use and to insist on taking them literally can be foolish pedantry. (It would hardly do to maintain that all manufactured goods were made by hand.) So inevitably I must conform and talk about borrowing, though I think myself that for this purpose adoption is the better word.

Alien words have been taken into our speech in so many different ways and at such different dates and have penetrated to such different depths that they can hardly in any case be lumped together under one label. Some that are new arrivals, like the popular Italian pizza, float lightly on the surface of our speech and may blow away at the next change of wind. More firmly established, though still obviously Italian, is spaghetti, which we may now use sometimes beyond the subject of food, talking, for instance, of a spaghetti junction. But both are still clearly foreign words for foreign commodities. How different the words that we took in the Middle Ages and have spelt and pronounced in English style so long that we have forgotten they were ever foreign, words like table and chair, dinner and supper, these are the real adoptions.

Often these adopted words have been changed in meaning as well as in form to suit our own needs and fancies. Think, for instance, of the word travel and what we have done to it; and, come to that, the French from whom we got it have changed it too. It is, of course, identical with their *travailler*, to work. It is derived from the late Latin name of a nasty three-pronged instrument (as brandished by devils in Last Judgement scenes) from which the French inherited a verb meaning to torture or later to be tortured or suffer pain. This we borrowed from them at an early date as 'travail' and continued to use in this painful sense, especially for 'women travailing of child', though that is very old-fashioned now. Meanwhile the same word, with modified sound and spelling, went on to a much more cheerful existence as travel.

How and why did the French in the course of time equate suffering with work and we with going abroad?

This is an oddity. One can see a reasonable link between suffering and work, and French peasants though industrious by nature did toil painfully hard, but the English have always been enthusiastic travellers and still are, from Chaucer's jolly company of pilgrims to the happy patrons of package tours today. And it is, I believe, in the thought of pilgrimages that the key to this change of meaning may be found, for the Middle English period when this word was picked up from abroad was the very heyday of this kind of enterprise.

For ordinary people who wanted to see something of the world a pilgrimage was almost the only way to set about it. From the time the English became Christian many of the more pious of them had gone to Rome, and once the Crusades had opened up the way to Jerusalem thousands made the long and arduous journey (not all of them so pious either), travelling in large parties and joined by others as they went along, mostly French, for a large part of their journey lay through France. There must have been great hardships to be endured *en route* and some dreadful mishaps, which would be told and retold in both languages with complaints and lamentations. When they came home the pilgrims could live on these stories for ever, using all the new expressions they had learned, and somehow the French word for suffering and toiling became indelibly associated with long journeys.

And yet most of the pilgrims enjoyed their adventures. The Wife of Bath certainly did for she went three times to Jerusalem besides numerous other places in Europe, and she was a jolly woman who loved her fun. 'Well coude she laughe in fellawshipe and carp.'

Another word probably picked up in much the same way was journey, from the French *journée* which means a day. It could also be used for a day's work or a day's march or ride, and may have been used in this way for a stage on a pilgrimage from one hostelry to the next. Again, the English were vague about its meaning and for them it became, like travel, synonymous with covering great distances. No time limit on a journey for us.

To the French themselves neither of these words ever meant travel. Their own word was *voyage* and in our omniverous way we have taken this too, but confined it to sea travel. It is clear that medieval excursionists came home with their speech larded with Gallicisms, many of them used incorrectly, but eagerly repeated as the right thing to say, just as today if you have had a trip to East Africa you must talk of going on safari. And one might well wonder what word the English had of their own for travelling before all these new-fangled words came in. They had 'wayfaring' or 'seafaring' or simply 'faring' from the Old English *faran*, to go far. This verb, to fare, is archaic now as a separate word but survives in several compounds such as farewell, thoroughfare and welfare (going on well). It is also alive in our fare on a bus or train which was originally our journey money. But the Wife of Bath and others of her sort regaling their friends with tales of foreign adventure were not going to use old-fashioned expressions when they knew the latest words, and so fare faded away before the onslaught of travel, journey and voyage.

These three words have long been English by any standard, the first two more deeply than voyage for it still looks like its French original and is not much different in meaning; the others are our own in all but origin. In fact any word adopted in the Middle English period (which ended in 1500) is as much integrated with our language as the descendants of a Frenchman who settled in England in Plantagenet times would be in our society.

As for words adopted before the Norman Conquest, it is absurd to think of them as even slightly alien, but all the same there is a fascination in discovering their roots and connecting them with our earliest known history. A familiar word like street, for instance, was learned from Romans—or from those who had heard it from Romans—when we were barbarians in their estimation and Latin still a living language. How much closer a link that is with ancient Rome than the Latin-isms adopted wholesale in modern times, words like referendum which is so palpably foreign to us that we can't decide how to make it plural. The Anglo-Saxons had no self-conscious problems of this sort. If they picked up a foreign word at all, which they didn't do often in their early days, they pronounced it in their own way and treated it as their own.

Adopted words of all periods are on the whole more sophisticated than the natives, dealing more with the trappings and accessories of life than with its essentials. As I look about me now, my table and chair, paper and pen, cushion, curtains and carpet are all named by adopted nouns, some of them very exotic too, for the paper comes from an Egyptian reed (*papyrus*) and the pen from an Italian feather (*penna*), but my own hands and eyes and thoughts and the warmth and the light are natives. But this is mere foolishness for I have just been picking out nouns from my surroundings, and speech is made of much more than nouns. Besides, one should avoid confusing the thing with the word. Thought is

50

an English word but if I call my thoughts ideas that is Greek.

Verbs, like nouns, are fairly equally divided between natives and adoptions, though all the most vital ones are English. But when we come to the lesser words, such as pronouns, prepositions and conjunctions that build words into sentences and make sense of them, these are practically all English. The thousands of foreign words we have taken into our vocabulary have given it colour and contrast and richness of texture, and endless subtle shades of meaning that it would never have had without them, but the basic structure of every sentence remains English.

If someone at this moment should look in and ask, 'What are you doing this evening?', and I answer, 'I'm working at my book about words but I'm not getting on as fast as I should like', the entire exchange would be of Anglo-Saxon origin. Try to say it in loan-words and you can't even begin.

2   The Early Period

The English were not always gluttons for other people's words. When the Angles and Saxons had spread as far over Britain as they were able to go, they settled down to be exclusively themselves for a very long time and their language—which varied not very greatly between the different tribes—replenished itself chiefly from its own resources. Being well satisfied with the land they had won, they put down deep roots, developing a culture and character distinctively their own, and this self-sufficiency is reflected in their vocabulary.

The English of today are often criticised for their insularity and that is a trait that showed itself very early. Of course the word 'insular' is wrong for the Anglo-Saxons unless used metaphorically, for they never occupied the whole island. By about the year 600, after two centuries of fighting, they had reached the western coasts at the estuaries of the Severn and the Dee, penning the Britons into Cornwall, Wales and Cumbria, and had pushed as far north as Edinburgh against more Britons, Gaels and Picts. There followed a slow penetration of Cornwall and Cumbria; Offa built his dyke as an admission that the Britons could keep Wales, while the northern border fluctuated back and forth; but from the early seventh century England was roughly established, and its language, with dialect variations, was English.

It is the presence of these other races in close proximity, particularly the Britons with whom there was most contact, and the fact that the English picked up hardly any of their words, that best illustrates their self-sufficiency in speech. They did adopt British place-names in large numbers, especially in the west—and this alone proves the contact—but that is quite a different matter from taking over common words to use in their own way. As they advanced they needed names for each new feature of the landscape that came in sight and if captured Britons could supply them, so much the better, but the way the invaders used these Celtic words shows how little they understood them. When a Briton pointing to a river said *afon* they received it as a name and called that river Avon ever after, clearly having no notion that it was the common word 'river', as it still is in Welsh.

It is clear to all who have studied the period that numbers of Britons must have continued to live in their old haunts after the English had overrun them, perhaps in some sort of servitude, but there seems to have been little conversation between the two races except about the lie of the land as if the newcomers were forever asking the way. The Britons so cut off from their compatriots probably learned English quickly. They were already partly bilingual, for during the long Roman occupation many of them must have spoken some Latin, and those who grow up with two languages are generally better able to master another than those who hear only one. And here is another characteristic that the English seem to have had from the start. They have never been good linguists. They expect other people to learn English, and this has been done to a remarkable extent. Such Britons as remained on English territory certainly did; so did the Danes who later settled in the northern region, though they had considerable influence on the speech around them; so also did the proud Normans in the end. So also in later times have countless others of many races overseas.

Of the handful of Celtic words the English invaders did pick up, nearly all were local and have remained so, like coombe for a narrow valley (Welsh *cwm*) which is used only in the west, and tor for a rocky prominence, but only in Devon. But a few Latin words that were probably learned from the Britons proved more generally useful, particularly port, wall and street from the Latin *portus*, *vallum* and *via strata*.

These three referred to phenomena for which the English had no words of their own. They would draw up their long boats on any beach without special equipment, and the remains of Roman harbours with stone wharves and storehouses were a novelty needing a name. Again, they protected their villages with only wooden stockades or prickly hedges, and the high Roman walls of dressed stone that stood around the abandoned cities must have seemed to them extraordinary, not to mention the great northern wall that stretched from sea to sea. And the roads also needed their special word.

It should be remembered that though the Roman Empire had covered most of Europe, it had never reached as far north as the forests of Saxony and Angeln (the narrow neck from which Denmark juts up), the regions from which these invading tribes had come. They had probably heard of the famous roads that the Romans had laid across Europe and may have known the word *strata* (which means paved) before they left the mainland, but it was only now in Britain that they had such things to call their own. At first they used the word for any Roman road, as is evident from the names of their settlements beside such roads—all those Stratfords, Strattons and Strettons—but gradually as long stretches of the highways fell into disuse, so the Latin word in its English form came to be used more in towns where, if the place was of Roman origin, the paving remained more visible.

'Street' has long had an urban character while the Old English 'road', once only a forest trackway, has taken its place for long-distance routes. Street, wall and port, that useful trio, are in a way more indigenous to Britain than the English, for they were here first, used by Romans and Britons in the same places.

This picking up of Latin words was the beginning of a long process, for we have been doing it ever since, in fits and starts according to the fashion of the time, and at the present time perhaps more than ever.

On the whole the Anglo-Saxons were allergic to foreign words and when new experiences came their way would express them in their own language as far as possible. When St Augustine came from Rome to convert them to Christianity, they took to it more readily than might have been expected and, the whole set up being new to them, did accept a certain amount of the Roman church vocabulary, such as bishop, abbot, priest, monk and nun. Actually all these words are Greek in origin, for the Romans were great borrowers from the Greek, but they arrived in England in Latin forms which the Saxons soon reduced to something like the modern words just given.

However, the Latin *ecclesia*—which Augustine and his monks must have used constantly, both for the organisation he founded and for the religious buildings under his direction—this word made no headway with the English. Instead they persisted in using a word of their own, *cirice* which we know as 'church'. The Old English spelling is confusing to the modern eye but if you bear in mind that 'c' followed by 'i' or 'e' was pronounced like our 'ch', you will see that it is the same word. Its origin has been much debated, but wherever it came from it was the Saxon word for a sacred place, and when the Roman missionaries spoke of the new building at Canterbury as *ecclesia* the local people kept on saying 'church'. It was many centuries later that such Latin derivatives as 'ecclesiastic' were to edge their way in.

Most of the religious words of classical origin that we know so well—Bible, testament, scripture, saint, and so on—came into England under Norman influence after the Conquest. The Saxons called all the Christian writings *god spell* (now gospel), good news in their language, and an evangelist was a *god spellere*. For the Latin *sanctus* their words were blessed, holy, or hallowed, and these they continued to use.

As for the Christian deity, the merciful father so different from the old heathen gods with their tricks and wiles, the missionaries called him *Deus* (which in French became *Dieu*), but the Saxons stuck firmly to their own word, God, the same that they had used for Thunor, Woden, Tiw and the rest. The Greek name Christ they did accept, for the coming of Christ was the essence of the good news, and immediately they began coining new words from it, such as christening

55

and Christendom, using their own suffixes to create words that were entirely English in character; while the *Spiritus Sanctus* was translated by that purely English expression, 'the Holy Ghost'.

Again, in regard to the feasts of the Christian church the Saxons showed their verbal independence. In late Latin the first day of the week had become the Lord's Day, *Dies Dominica* (which in French became *Dimanche*) but the English maintained their old allegiance to the sun; and the culmination of the Christian year, Easter, still bears the name of a heathen fertility goddess, Eostre, whose festival was held at about that time.

But though the early English had little tendency to absorb foreign words into their language, it would be wrong to suggest that they disliked Latin. They respected it as the key to knowledge, the gateway to the wider world, feeling just as many Asians and Africans and others in foreign lands feel now about English. The first important book written by an Englishman, Bede's history of the English church, finished at Jarrow in 731, was written in Latin as a matter of course. It was copied and admired beyond England which could not have happened if he had used his native tongue.

In the next century Alfred, writing to one of his bishops, lamented that so few of his people could then read Latin. But his plan to improve matters was not only to found a school to teach it, which he did, but also to have as many books as possible translated into English. One of the first he chose was Bede's history which we thus have in ninth-century English as well as Latin. Other books dealt with religion and general knowledge as far as it went at that time. More importantly, Alfred's new idea and his industry in carrying it out made English prose a literary language in its own right.

I stress prose because the composing of poetry was a deep-rooted habit of the English from before our first records begin. Bede in his account of the poetic cowherd, Caedmon, shows vividly a society where to extemporise in rhythmic,

56

poetic words to the music of the harp was a normal manly accomplishment and to fail at it was shameful. Poetry was then not for the few but for all, and enough has survived from that time to show its imaginative quality and its sensitivity to the sounds of words. It used many words that were even then archaic for they are not found in the prose of that time, a clear indication of an old tradition of native poetry. A short example is given on page 135.

But prose was another thing, at first purely utilitarian, useful for stating laws or making grants of land, until Alfred raised it to higher purposes. From his reign the great Anglo-Saxon Chronicle, which before that was only a scrappy list of brief facts, takes on a more literary character, and owing largely to the impetus he gave it, it continued to be kept long after his death, covering over three hundred years of the ups and downs of the English people told in their own contemporary words. No other modern European language has anything comparable. It ends sadly in 1154 after Stephen's execrable reign, and with it ended the writing of pure Old English.

3 In Middle English

With the Norman Conquest the strong tide of alien words began to flow into England. Not a flood all at once, for the English people, stunned by what had happened to them, continued to speak their own tongue unadulterated for a long time before the French words that they heard around them began to take effect. But the ultimate effect was very great.

England before this had been not only independent but aloof. Now it was linked with Europe. The ruling classes went back and forth to their continental possessions and in due course numbers of Englishmen employed in their large retinues of soldiers and servants went with them. They fought in French wars, went on Crusades, and came home bilingual. New monasteries were founded and the church was an international network. A clever young man who could speak French and write Latin could go anywhere.

At home for the main body of the English, tied to the land, the unfamiliar language which their new masters talked was a sinister cloud hanging over them which could up to a point be ignored but not completely. New landlords ruled over them with whom the leaders of each community—their own authority much diminished—must communicate. The respected title 'thane' vanished from the vocabulary, though 'lord' and 'earl' survived triumphantly, adopted by the victors alongside their own 'baron'. Duke William was glad enough to assume the English title of 'king', but for his sons the French 'prince' took the place of the Old English 'atheling'. The worst insult came to the honourable old word, churl, which had signified a free peasant owning his own land. Churlish remains as a form of abuse, a nasty hangover from Norman racism.

Shires became counties, and the old moot which had formerly regulated local affairs was replaced by a manor court. Court was another word which had come to stay, and has developed in several directions, varying from the royal household to a place to play tennis. The Witan, which meant 'wise men', was abolished, replaced eventually by a parliament—literally a talking, or discussion, group. But occasionally an English word picked up by the Normans—even in the highest circles—found a place in the affairs of state, as for example 'bench', used collectively for the chief judges who sat together on this homely article.

Some words are forced upon one by circumstances whether one likes them or not. We in England are now obliged to talk of metres, litres and kilos however unnatural they seem, even hectares, though that seems impossible when one looks at the ancient pattern of the landscape, created by men who ploughed in acres for fifteen hundred years. But the children already take it all for granted. In the eleventh century no attempt was made to interfere with such primitive matters, nor with the native coinage: shillings and pence, already centuries old, were allowed to continue, but there were some new words to learn in suffering, such as castle, dungeon and prison.

Castle comes from the Latin *castellum*, a little fort, which in Norman French was *castel*, and the English word is much closer to the original than the modern French equivalent. One of the local characteristics of Norman French was the retention of the Latin hard 'c' which in central France had already changed to a soft 'ch'. Old French was at this time in a very fluid state with even more sound-changes taking place than in English. A medial 's' was generally dropped before 't' and the ending '-el' regularly became '-eau'. So in standard French, *castel* became *château*; and the sense altered too as life grew more civilised, so that the word that had begun as a grim fortress now serves in France for any fine, large residence. Not so in England where the castle has remained strictly defensive, and where the nobility, once the need for fortification was gone, reverted to the old native word, 'house', for their splendid homes. Some of their

59

'country houses' might well be called palaces, but that is a word we use very sparingly.

The English under the Normans gradually learned such new words as they had to know, but kept their own too. This resulted in many pairs of words for the same thing, but with different shades of meaning, making an overall gain in subtlety. The Saxon peasant in the fields still spoke of bulls, cows, calves, sheep and swine—or he might say pigs—but the servants in the castle who set cooked meat before the gentry must use the French words, which have come down to us as beef, veal, mutton and pork. In France the same word serves for the animal whether alive or on your plate.

In much the same way the English continued naturally to use their native verbs 'walk' and 'sing'. They also learned the French equivalents, *marcher* and *chanter*, but restricted each to a special use, marching for soldiers, chanting for monks, both organised and formal while our own words remain free. We gained two precise new meanings here which the French lack, for their soldiers must walk even on parade.

The English people learned French words at first because they had to, and later because they began to like them, but the mass of the people have never learned a second language and probably never will. The demise of French as a spoken language in England, except at court, was hastened by the loss of nearly all the Norman kings' possessions in France at the end of King John's reign. With those gone the distinction between Norman and English seemed to vanish too. In the following century, English kings led successful armies against the French, armies in which king, nobles, knights and common men-at-arms shared the same loyalty. On a wave of national revival the English language came into its own, and in 1362 its victory was ratified by an Act of Parliament making it the official language of the law. When you consider how strongly lawyers resist change and love their ancient phraseology, you can realise what a triumph this was for the native tongue.

Of course the influx of French words didn't stop. On the contrary it increased greatly, for now that racial tension was eased and the mental barrier broken down, French words became all the fashion, the in-words of their day. About this time England produced her first great poet, Chaucer. He is typical of the up-and-coming men of that day, familiar with court life and the world of business, widely travelled in Europe, fluent in French as well as English, and yet choosing to write in English enriched with words from other sources. For there were other languages besides French from which pickings could be taken. The ever-increasing influence of the church offered countless possibilities from Latin and Greek, and there was yet another source of vocabulary in medieval England that must not be forgotten, Danish.

The Danes, who had settled in England before the Conquest as ruthless enemies, were by the twelfth century living peaceably among the English. Under the shock of the Norman domination the former enemies suffered equal disabilities, and no doubt adversity drew them together. As a separate language Danish seems to have disappeared quickly, blending into English in a way that French could never do, but not without making its contribution, especially in the north.

Danish and northern English were so much alike to start with that often the Scandinavian influence was only a matter of pronunciation, but significant none the less, as in the case of the homely word, egg. In Middle English this was *ei*. It had earlier ended with a guttural sound (the one that often appears in our spelling as 'gh'), but that had gone and the word was in danger of being confused with 'eye'. But in Danish the corresponding word ended in a firm, hard 'g' which made it quite distinctive. Northerners began to use this form and it slowly spread southwards, reaching the southern counties only after 1500.

Something similar happened to our plural pronouns. If it were not for Danish influence we might still be saying 'hey' and 'hem' for 'they' and 'them'. Perhaps it wouldn't have mattered, but with vowels so apt to change the English plurals had become dangerously close to the singular 'he' and 'him', and this was a difference that needed preserving for the sake of clarity. The initial 'th' borrowed from the equivalent Danish pronouns served the purpose, and was easily adopted as many English words began with this sound. We see the transition in Chaucer who used both forms:

> The holy blisful martir for to seke,
> That hem hath holpen, whan that they were seke.

There were also words borrowed in the north that were purely Scandinavian, especially those that relate to the scenery, such as beck, gill, dale and fell. All these remain exclusively northern. It would show great ignorance to use them in describing the South Downs or Exmoor.

But some Danish words were fully accepted into the standard language and that means that they have now gone round the world. One is the essential 'leg'. Previously the English spoke of the thigh (or alternatively the ham), while shank served for the lower part of the limb. But a more comprehensive word was a convenience and the Danish one was adopted.

Another very basic word of Danish origin is 'sky'. How, one wonders, could the Anglo-Saxons ever have managed without it? But of course they had their own word, several in fact, the one they used most being heaven (OE *heofon*). It was, I believe, the effect of Christianity that made them feel the need for something else. Imagining God to be somewhere vaguely on high they used 'heaven' to translate *paradisus*, and then the religious significance outweighed its ordinary meaning. So in time plain men, looking upward for signs of coming weather, began to use the short, uncomplicated word that they heard from their Danish neighbours. We can still use heaven (or 'the heavens') for sky if so inclined, but it does seem over-poetical.

62

The English had hated and resented the invasions of their country by Danes and Normans, but in the long run the language benefited greatly from both. Of the two influences that of French is far the greater, and with it Latin, because French being descended from Latin, it is often impossible to say whether a word comes from one or the other. You might say that the Norman Conquest and the consequent influx of French and Latin words (including Greek words that came by way of Latin) doubled our vocabulary, but that is not quite true, for all the familiar words that we use most often are still English. However, it has doubled our choice of nouns, verbs, and adjectives, the theme-words of our speech, and it is this wide variety of synonyms, combined with our very simple grammar, that has given English its great flexibility, and in the hands of a master its musical quality. Our wealth of words means that a writer or speaker can choose the one he wants not only for exact meaning and emotional tone, but also for length, weight and rhythm.

And although our copious borrowing has resulted in dozens of pairs of words whose meanings are literally the same, yet their background associations have given each one its special character so that perfect synonyms are rare. Liberty and freedom, riches and wealth, actions and deeds—these pairs are almost identical, but even so there are slight undertones of difference that the sensitive mind will feel. In most cases the adopted word is more formal than the native and often positively pompous. Sufficient may mean the same as enough, but still sounds alien; commence is pretentious compared with begin, and imbibe absurd beside drink. But occasionally the French word, if it was adopted early, has proved a winner in this verbal rivalry. Flower is one that we could not now do without. It has relegated the Old English blossom to flowering trees, and we can gladly use both words. People, too, has had a big success, quite defeating the English word folk which is now confined to a special old-world context. French marriage and English wedding are still running neck and neck, but the verb to marry has got the better of wed which is now quaint.

I find it intriguing to play off such pairs against each other, awarding the prizes according to my own preference. Or one can make a team game of it. On a cheerful note French might put forward joy, delight, gaiety, jollity and pleasure, while English counters with happiness, mirth, glee, cheerfulness and bliss, all good players with further reserves that might be called up. On the opposite theme French could field grief, distress, regret, misery and anguish, and English reply with sorrow, sadness, unhappiness, woe and pain.

Of course when I speak of French and English in these imaginary contests, I am referring to origins only. All those words are English now, the French ones long ago knocked into shape to suit English ears and eyes. Delight, for instance, (OF *delit*) has even had an English 'gh' stuffed into it as if it were related to 'light', which it is not, and as an adjective it carries the English suffix -ful without the least hint of incongruity. In return many English words have taken French endings, such as merriment, which I did not include in either team as it belongs in part to each of them.

Certainly we have a wealth of words, or shall I say a profusion, or an abundance, or a plethora.

4   *Since 1500*

Modern English is officially dated from 1500. In general we think of the speech of the Tudor period as decidedly old-fashioned and certainly when we talk of modern English with a small 'm' we don't mean anything like that. But for those who study the language the three main divisions are very distinct: Old English, the foundations; Middle English, the time of transition; and Modern English when the language as we know it has taken shape.

These divisions reflect real events that shaped men's lives as well as their speech. The Norman Conquest was a hard fact, and round about 1500 many things were happening to change men's mental outlook. One was the renaissance of classical learning which had just reached England, another the discovery of the New World, but the most significant for our purpose was the invention of printing.

When Caxton set up his printing press in Westminster in 1477 it was, as we might say in modern parlance, the first appearance of 'the media'. Of all the Latin words that have flowed into England in recent times, few have attained more sudden popularity with less general grasp of their nature than media. There was need for a single word for 'means of mass communication', including newspapers and radio, but since the most potent of these is now television, 'media' has become more attached to that than to anything else. I know a woman who calls her set the media ('I'll just turn off the media') and it may come to that. Then there is the question whether it is singular or plural. It is of course a plural noun in Latin, but that is unlikely to signify much. The general public will decide for itself.

I suppose it would be agreed that after the development of speech itself the next step in the progress of the 'media' was the invention of writing, but important though that was, its influence grew only slowly and was very limited in scope. Before the coming of printing, few books had been written

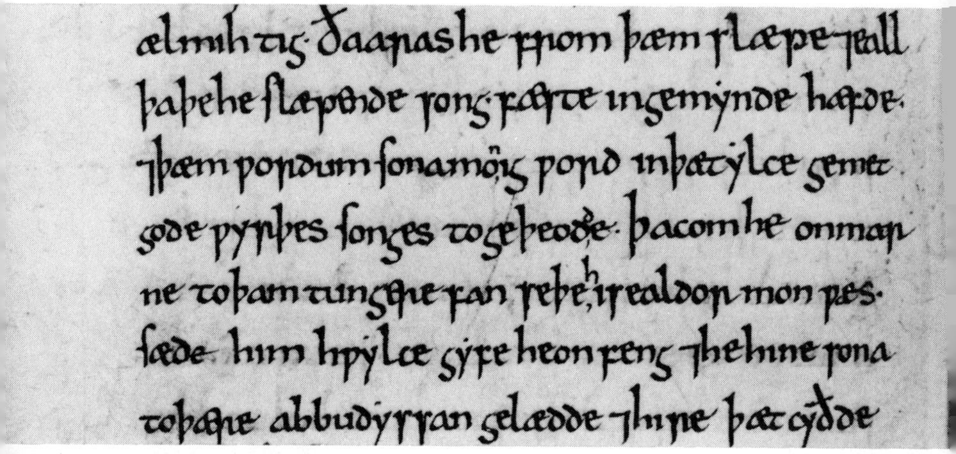
ælmihtig· Ða aras he from þæm slæpe ⁊ eall
þa þe he slæpende song fæste in gemynde hæfde·
⁊ þæm wordum sona monig word in þæt ylce gemet
Gode wyrþes songes togeþeodde· Þa com he on mar
ne to þam tungerefan se þe his ealdormon wæs·
sæde him hwylce gyfe he onfeng ⁊ he hine sona
to þære abbudyssan gelædde ⁊ hire þæt cyðde

Fig. 1 Part of the MS of Bede's *Historia Ecclesiastica*, as translated into English at King Alfred's court.

This looks much more obscure than it really is, owing to the Anglo-Saxon script, which included several characters (notably those for 'th' and 'w') which disappeared centuries ago. Another difficulty in this MS is the frequent lack of spaces between words. Translated into modern type, it is instantly more recognisable.

The first word, *ælmihtig* (almighty) is the last word of the hymn which Caedmon composed in a dream. The MS continues:

> . . . .Tha aras he from tham slæpe, and eall
> tha the he slæpende song fæste in gemynde hæfde,
> and tham wordum sona monig word in that ylce gemet
> Gode wyrthes songes togetheodde. Tha com he on mar-
> ne to tham tun gerefan, se the his ealdormon wæs,
> sæde him hwylce gyfe he onfeng, and he hine sona
> to thære abbudyssan gelædde, and hire thæt cythde.

This may be modernised, word for word, as follows:

> . . . .Then arose he from that sleep, and all
> that that he sleeping sang fast in mind had,
> and [to] those words soon many words in that same metre
> [of that] God-worthy song togethered. Then came he in mor-
> n to the town reeve, he that his alderman was,
> [and] said [to] him which gift he had received, and he him soon
> to the abbess led, and [to] her [all] that made known.

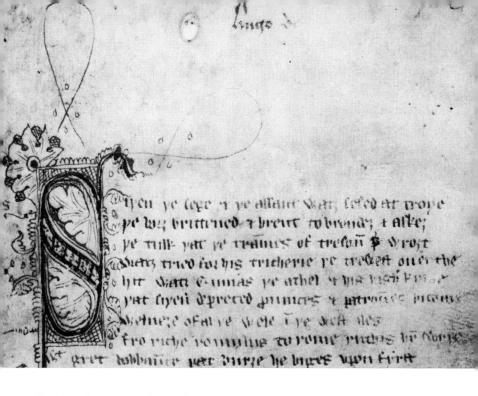

Fig. 2 The opening lines of a narrative poem, known as *Sir Gawain and the Green Knight*, and believed to have been written between 1375 and 1400, at about the same time as Chaucer's *Canterbury Tales*. Unlike Chaucer, who rhymed the ends of lines (as may be seen in Figure 4, overleaf) and who wrote in the East Midlands dialect of London and the home counties, this anonymous poet followed the old tradition of alliteration (see Appendix 1, page 135) and used the dialect of Cheshire and south Lancashire, with its high proportion of consonants, giving a harsher bonier sound to the verse and a sharp edge to passages of description.

Translated into modern type, the lines run as follows:

Sithen the sege and the assaut   was cesed at Troye,
The borgh brittened and brent   to brondes and askes,
The tulk that the trammes   of tresoun ther wroght
Was tried for his tricherie,   the trewest on erthe.
Hit was Ennias the athel   and his highe kynde,
That sithen depreced provinces,   and patrounes bicome
Welneghe of all the wele   in the West Iles.

tulk = man   trammes = schemes, cunning plans
depreced = subdued   wele = wealth

Fig. 3 William Caxton's patron, Anthony Woodville, Earl Rivers, presents to his brother-in-law, Edward IV, the first book printed in England. This was *Dictes and Sayenges of the Phylosophers*, which Rivers had translated into 'right good and fayr Englyssh'.

Caxton himself had begun his literary career as a translator, copying out his work by hand. In March 1469, when he was living in the Low Countries in the service of Edward IV's sister, the Duchess of Burgundy, he began translating the *Recuyell of the Historyes of Troye*. By the time he finished it, in September 1471, his pen, he said, was worn, 'his hand weary, his eye dimmed' by all the copying. He decided to learn about printing at the Cologne presses, where printers were producing Latin and Greek texts, and in 1475 he published his translation of the *Recuyell* in Bruges. Returning to England the following year, he set up his press at the sign of the Red Pale in the city of Westminster, where *Dictes and Sayenges* appeared on November 18, 1477.

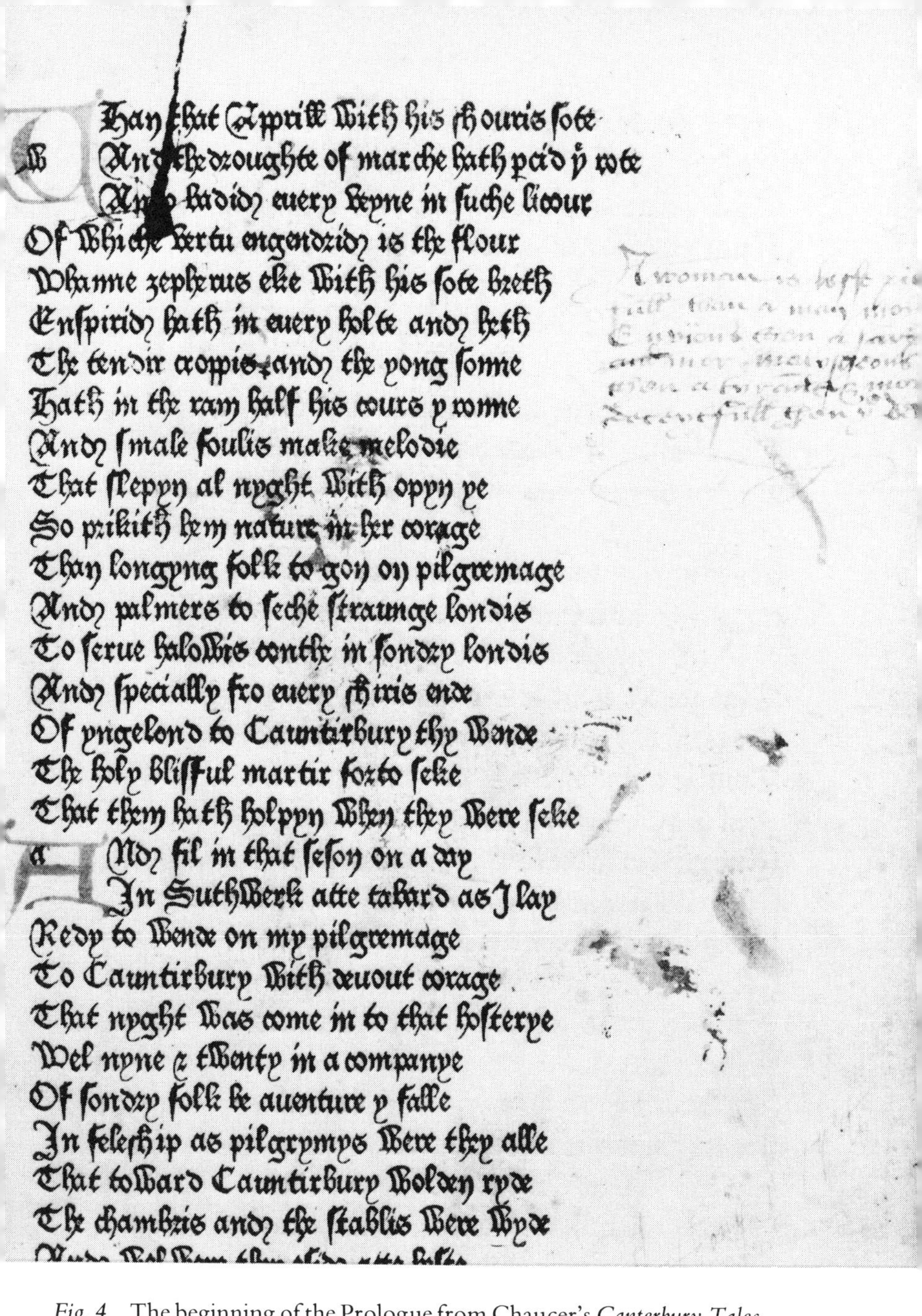
Whan that Apprill with his shouris sote
And the droughte of marche hath percid ye rote
And badid every veyne in suche licour
Of which vertu engendrid is the flour
Whanne zepherus eke with his sote breth
Enspirid hath in every holte and heth
The tendir croppis and the yong sonne
Hath in the ram half his cours y ronne
And smale foulis make melodie
That slepyn al nyght with opyn ye
So prikith hem nature in her corage
Than longyng folk to goon on pilgremage
And palmers to seke straunge londis
To serve halowis couthe in sondry londis
And specially fro every shiris ende
Of yngelond to Cauntirbury they wende
The holy blisful martir forto seke
That them hath holpyn whan they were seke
And fil in that seson on a day
In Suthwerk atte tabard as I lay
Redy to wende on my pilgremage
To Cauntirbury with devout corage
That nyght was come in to that hosterye
Wel nyne & twenty in a companye
Of sondry folk be aventure y falle
In feleship as pilgrymys were they alle
That toward Cauntirbury wolden ryde
The chambris and the stablis were wyde

Fig. 4 The beginning of the Prologue from Chaucer's *Canterbury Tales*, printed by Caxton at his press in Westminster.

A

DICTIONARY

OF THE

ENGLISH LANGUAGE:

IN WHICH

THE WORDS ARE DEDUCED FROM THEIR ORIGINALS,

AND

ILLUSTRATED IN THEIR DIFFERENT SIGNIFICATIONS,

BY

EXAMPLES FROM THE BEST WRITERS.

TO WHICH ARE PREFIXED,

A HISTORY OF THE LANGUAGE,

AND AN

ENGLISH GRAMMAR.

BY SAMUEL JOHNSON, L.L.D.

IN TWO VOLUMES.

VOL. I.

Cum tabulis animum censoris sumet honesti ;
Audebit quaecunque parum splendoris habebunt,
Et sine pondere erunt, et honore indigna ferentur,
Verba movere loco ; quamvis invita recedant,
Et versentur adhuc intra penetralia Vestae.
Obscurata diu populo bonus eruet, atque
Proferet in lucem speciosa vocabula rerum,
Quae priscis memorata Catonibus atque Cethegis
Nunc situs informis premit, et deserta vetustas.   Hor.

LONDON;
PRINTED BY JOHN JARVIS, AND SOLD BY JOHN FIELDING, No. 23, PATERNOSTER-ROW.
MDCCLXXXVI.

Fig. 5 The title page of Dr Johnson's *Dictionary*. This edition, with a portrait of him, was published shortly after his death.

Fig. 6 Sir James Murray, first editor and chief compiler of the *Oxford English Dictionary*, in his 'scriptorium'.

or read in English. Tales, ballads and information were passed on largely orally, their wording being constantly adjusted to current speech. Now there was a sudden impetus to write histories, poems and plays in the vernacular and to translate them from other languages, the exact words of the authors being preserved and multiplied. Now schools were founded in every sizeable town and schoolboys, creeping like snails unwillingly (but some were glad of it afterwards), had the wonders of classical literature crammed into them. Now theatres were built, fashionable young men wrote poetry, and the native literature blossomed amazingly.

The new medium of the printed word, like the more potent media of today, had two opposite influences on the language, the one tending towards uniformity, for the setting up of a standard always diminishes local differences, and the other towards a rapid spread of new words and ways of using them. Today a television personality has only to use a new expression and it is taken up immediately by millions. Effects were not caused so rapidly by Elizabethan books and plays, but none the less they were great. The language was at once steadied on its foundations and enriched with new material.

Londoners of that time seem to have been drunk with words. The audiences from all ranks of society who crammed the theatres must have revelled in long rhetorical speeches or the successful young dramatists would not have filled their plays with them. Shakespeare, raised above the others by his genius, was only one of many. If printing led the media of that time, the theatre came second.

The new words that poured in now were mostly from Latin or Greek, no longer through religious channels, but direct from the classical fount. No doubt they were as exciting to the young intellectuals as the new coinages of scientific technology are to the young of today, all those nymphs and heroes, all those -isms and -ologies, and all the specialised jargon of the playhouse—drama, tragedy, prologue, dialogue, scenes, chorus, and of course theatre itself, all new in that century.

Shakespeare was no great scholar but he was like a sponge where words were concerned and could make them serve him, adding a suffix here, a prefix there, using a noun as a verb or vice versa as his rapidly flowing ideas or the rhythm of the line required. Many familiar words appear first in his plays in the guise in which we know them, but one can't say for certain that this or that one was his creation, for he may have heard it first in a nobleman's household or among the scholars of the law courts, or from any of the drunken company in a Cheapside tavern.

When Hamlet speaks of man as the 'paragon of animals' he is using two new words from the world of scholarship, paragon straight from the Greek, animal from the Latin *animalis*. This was the adjective of *anima*, the breath of life or the spirit. Shakespeare uses it as a plural noun to imply all living creatures. It still had far to go before it would vie with and eventually overcome the Old English 'beast' in popular speech. Animal never appears in the King James Bible where beast still reigns unchallenged. But gradually the new word triumphed and beast survives only in old-fashioned and diminished style. (Strange that a nation of animal lovers should have made such a derogatory adjective from it.)

From the founding of the Tudor grammar schools right through to the present century, English education was so firmly based on the study of the classics that the stream of words from these two languages has never ceased, and though they have now almost disappeared from our schools their influence on our conversation has not dwindled. Indeed it seems to increase. We call them dead languages because they are not spoken any more, but they are like the man in the song who is dead but he won't lie down. And the same children who rejoice that they don't have to learn Latin, describe the size of things as *maxi-* or *mini-*, are glad to get *bonus* marks and acclaim everything as *super*.

73

Until the eighteenth century many of our leading scholars wrote Latin as easily as English. The greatest of them, Newton, propounded his *Principia Mathematica* in Latin as a matter of course and both before and since his time the technical terms of all the sciences have been made of Latin and Greek material.

For it is not so much whole words of classical origin as the endless prefixes and suffixes that have such irrepressible life. They form a pool of spare parts for building up the long words in which all too many members of learned and official bodies like to clothe their utterances. Some people prefer short words but there are others, particularly in public life, who think that extra syllables add dignity, and for them the classical affixes form an inexhaustible supply of building material. You can, for instance, institute something. That much is simple, the nub of it being *-stit-* which is part of the Latin *statuere*, to set up. What you have set up is now an institution and may be described as institutional. Then with the aid of another classical suffix you can institutionalise something else, and this act can be referred to as institutionalisation. Personally I am anti-institutionalisation, not because I object to Latin suffixes and prefixes, but they should be used with moderation, and there should be a law against having -tion twice in one word. But there are no rules in this game.

I must come back to the language of officialdom later. For the moment it is pleasanter to return to the first Elizabethans, those exuberant people who loved words and used them with a marvellous instinct. (Elizabeth herself was an inspired speaker, a fine scholar and linguist, but one who made her best effects with simple English words.) They took them not only from the classics but also from all the living languages of Europe with which they had much contact, and the process was continued by their descendants, particularly in the realm of the arts. In the seventeenth and eighteenth centuries, most of the English nobility were rebuilding their houses and Italian styles were all the rage. Gentlemen who made the grand tour came home full of notions of porticoes, frescoes, vistas and the like, and all the proper words for them. The opera, too, was new to them and gradually the whole language of music was imported from Italy.

Holland also had its influence, especially in the field of painting. Dutch artists were made welcome by the Stuart kings and left as a legacy such words as sketch, landscape and easel. There were also contacts with them on the sea, not always friendly, and from these the English picked up skipper, sloop, deck and yacht. Note how close the Dutch words are to the English. Skipper is the same word as shipper, just slightly different in sound and meaning. If landscape had developed in English, it would have been landship.

English admiration for French culture and style of living never waned, even during the long period from before 1700 to 1815 when the two countries were generally at war. Although the French were our enemies, their army was taken as a model and almost all military terms, such as the names of ranks, were faithfully reproduced. As for clothes, cookery and social amenities, French fashions prevailed, unchecked by any thought of hostility. Meanwhile the Americans, in alliance with the French at the end of this period, began borrowing from them quite separately on their own account.

But as we come to the nineteenth century, we can see a great change in the style of borrowing. In earlier times loanwords once adopted were generally totally anglicised both in spelling and pronunciation. The French *façon* (way or mode) became fashion with no nonsense about it. And look what happened to *peruque*, at first rendered as periwig and then shortened to wig. You can hardly say 'wig' is French. But the spread of general education has had the effect of making us keep the foreign appearance of newly borrowed words and a sort of rough approximation to their sound; seldom very successful, for in spite of the long association of French and English, neither side has ever found the other's language easy. It is really remarkable how many words we have in

75

common and how differently we say them. Look, for instance, at theatre, identical in writing but the second 't' is the only sound in the word that is the same in both languages. But whereas few English people outside the aristocracy used to make any attempt to say French words in a French way, we do all try now up to a point. With words like depot and debut it is easy not to sound the final consonant, but the vowel sounds are still beyond us.

Of course the whole business cuts both ways, for many English words are now fashionable in France, and the French find ours just as hard to pronounce as we find theirs.

You might think we would have reached saturation point by now, especially with so many new words coming from America, but more still come from France. To have a boutique is much smarter than keeping a shop, and politicians in speaking of better-relations-with-Russia are obliged to say detente as a convenience word for gliding over an awkward subject. Then they can only meet at a venue. This is tolerable when it is somewhere abroad with an international flavour, but why are footballers so fond of it, and for home matches too? It is dragged in so unnecessarily as if to raise the status of the game. 'Bootle is to play Tootle on Saturday but the venue where they will meet is not yet settled.' Oh, dear.

V

MORE ADOPTIONS

1 Borrowing the Same Word Twice

One reason why the habit of borrowing other people's words is such a great multiplier of vocabulary is that the same word can be borrowed twice, or any number of times, with a different result each time. That applies particularly to our borrowing from Europe where the Romans took words from the Greeks, the French and Italians inherited them from the Romans, and we picked them up from all or any of them at different dates and different levels of society and treated them in different ways once we had them.

For instance, spirit and sprite are the same in origin, the first direct from Latin, the second in a more popular form from France which took on quite a different character once it was here. Channel and canal are also the same, the one from France, the other from Italy. Hotel, hostel and hospital are all ultimately from the Latin *hospis*, a host. We have differentiated them nicely and can use them all, as well as hospitality, which is what we should logically expect from a hospital.

Fantasy and fancy both come from the Greek *phantasma*, with which phantom is also connected. Fantasy remains somewhat poetical, though its adjective is very popular, but fancy has been thoroughly taken to our hearts. We use it as noun, adjective or verb as the fancy takes us, and it has got into this sentence without my having intended it. Such a pleasant, easy word will creep in anywhere, and a little of what you fancy does you good.

Suit was adopted from France at an early date as a legal term. It came from the Latin *sequita*, a part of *sequere*, to follow, and was used at first for attendance at a law court;

77

in England it developed other varied meanings such as a suit of clothes; then much later it was readopted with French spelling and pronunciation as 'suite'. Suit and suite are obviously the same word but if you were to speak of wearing a suite of clothes or booking a suit of rooms it would be thought very odd. Sequence comes also from the same source.

You would never guess that ticket and etiquette share the same origin, but they do. Ticket, from the Old French *estiquet* (which was related to the English verb 'stick'), was current in Tudor England as a written notice stuck up in a public place, but later it came to be a smaller piece of paper which people could carry with them authorising them to do something, like travel on public transport. Meanwhile etiquette came into the English world of fashion in the mid-eighteenth century as a written list of rules which the master of ceremonies at a large function could refer to. Later it was just the rules.

Then there is paste. We borrowed it long ago as a mixture of a certain consistency, edible or not—more often not—and from that we made a verb concentrating chiefly on its sticking powers, and another verb in lower circles stressing the fact that the mixture had to be well beaten. ('I'll give you a pasting.') We also borrowed it as pasty (OF *pasté*) for a mixture of chopped meat contained in a casing made chiefly of flour, a favourite dish of medieval England and still so in Devon and Cornwall; and we imported it again as pastry for the floury mixture only, which has since been a great feature of English cookery. Meanwhile it continued in France as *pâté*, largely made of meat, and in Italy as *pasta*, largely made of flour, and although we have so much paste-ery of our own we have welcomed both of those as well, as they are all different forms of food, though derived from the one word. In ancient Rome it meant a medicinal lozenge, that presumably had been well pasted.

From the Latin *festus* with its adjective *festivus* comes a similar string of words acquired by us at various dates: feast, festival, festivity, fête and fiesta. Such a list illustrates the different degrees of absorption, fiesta being (like pasta) still a foreign word but one that is rapidly gaining in popularity. Fête is thoroughly integrated into our social life—all those village fêtes—but still looking foreign because we cling to the circumflex to show how cultured we are; and feast is deeply embedded in the language, its religious significance nearly lost in the pleasures of the table.

Two common words that you would never normally associate are direct and dress, yet both come from the Latin *directus*, the one in a perfectly straightforward way, the other deviously. In giving the origin of 'dress' you would have to say it is French, but we have developed it so freely on our own lines that its modern English meaning is all our own. It comes from the French verb *dresser* which is a contraction of the late Latin *directiare* (much modified in the usual French style). It means (in French) to stand up straight, get in line, put in order and generally prepare. It has no noun form except *dressage* which we know in connection with horses and which refers to their training. It has nothing to do with clothes. A dresser as a piece of furniture, an early borrowing, meant a side table on which food could be prepared or set out; it is only in English and in the theatre that it can also be a person to help you dress.

It was in seventeenth-century England that this word was first used in fashionable circles for the process of getting a person ready for the day's activities, just as food might be dressed for a banquet. It involved attention to the toilet, hair (or wig), and complexion, in fact the whole get-up for either sex. When Herrick praised a sweet disorder in the dress he meant the whole appearance which he liked natural—even a little untidy. Not till the second half of the nineteenth century was the noun associated with a particular garment worn by women and girls, a purely English usage and very recent. But the whole connection with clothes is an English invention.

It may be noted that the word address, whether noun or verb, has kept much closer to its origin. If you address yourself to someone you speak directly to him, and the address on a letter is a direction.

One more pair of words sprung surprisingly from the same origin is chair and cathedral. In ancient Greek, *cathedra* meant an ordinary chair, and as such passed through Latin into French, first as *chadiere*, then *chaire*, in which state it reached Norman England where the Saxons had hitherto been sitting on stools, benches or settles. (In France it changed further into *chaise*, but that doesn't concern us.) Meanwhile in early Christian Rome so much of the regular church vocabulary was Greek that *cathedra* had acquired a specialised meaning of a bishop's throne in a principal church, and during the reorganisation of the English church at the Reformation it was introduced, first as an adjective, a cathedral church being one with a bishop attached.

This brings us to a bishop's see, which is also—like a gentleman's country seat—the place where he sits or belongs. And now we must bring English into play as well as Latin and French to show something of the multiplicity of words that can grow from one root. The Old English *sittan* and the Latin *sedere* (both to sit) are cognate, both being descended from the same Indo-European root. Before the English came to Britain their verb had broken into two forms with the roots set- and sit-, expressing the transitive and intransitive forms of the same idea, either you could set something down or just sit yourself; and from set- a secondary verb developed, settle, which could be either. From these three closely related Old English verbs, we have a seat or a settle or a settee to sit on, a sitting (as of Parliament), a setting (as of a play or of jewels or of almost anything), a settling or a settlement (of money, or the crust of the earth, or of colonists in a new land).

From the Latin sed-, we have sediment or sedimentation (which has settled down), sedation (which makes you settle down), and a session, which is precisely a sitting; while from French, where the Latin root was reduced to no more than *se-*, we get the bishop's see, a seance and a siege, which last was a sitting around.

Here are fourteen nouns (I haven't troubled with other parts of speech) all stemming from the same root word expressing the simple act of sitting. And there are more too. If we were to start on all the meanings of set as a noun, it would be excessive, and some have wandered rather far from the original idea, though I can't forbear from mentioning a badger's sett because it tallies so nicely with the bishop's see and the country seat. But the point is that though English alone can muster so many words sprung from one root, the process of borrowing within the same family of languages can more than double the number.

Logically they should all have the same meaning but such is the nature of language that each has gathered special associations around it and no two are quite the same, some very different. So when a new kind of sitting takes place, as when a group of people decide to occupy a building in protest against something, they have to invent a new term and call it a sit-in, and that makes one more.

The nouns formed from the same root for the people who sit, set or settle have become very specialised. Settlers are not those who settle themselves on settles but pioneers in distant lands; setter is used chiefly for a breed of dog taught to stay set in one position; sitter in modern speech is generally a shortened form of baby-sitter, a useful phenomenon that has probably come to stay. Those who engage in sit-ins are known as sitters-in. They have much in common, both in their verbal origin and their intent, with besiegers, the only real difference being that one lot is inside and the other out.

2 Long-Range Borrowing

English has imported more words from Europe, especially from French, Latin and Greek, than from all the rest of the world put together. All the same, from the time of the Conquest onwards some words from further afield did reach England, chiefly—in the Middle Ages—from the mysterious lands of Asia, brought back by pilgrims, crusaders and enterprising merchants.

Nowadays with rapid world-wide communication we can pick up words from anywhere and use them at once in their native form if they happen to take our fancy: safari from East Africa, anorak from the Eskimos, judo and tycoon from Japan, sauna from Finland, all in fashion at the moment, but fashions can change so quickly it is never safe to predict which recently imported words will be gone again in a few years and which still here and thoroughly settled in.

Looking back at the older imports from exotic lands, we see that they could only come slowly across Europe, reaching English by way of Greek or Latin and then often through the medium of French, already much modified on the long journey. Many were lost on the way, but the skills and arts of the Moslem world and the dangers and delights to be found there proved talking points of endless fascination in a world whose excitements were more limited than ours. Arabic words that reached England in medieval times include alchemy, alcohol, and algebra (the al- is the definitive article which often adhered), assassin, arsenic, crimson, amber, lemon, cotton, syrup and sugar. Another is magazine which came to us meaning a storehouse, but in modern times has been used metaphorically as a 'storehouse' of literary items.

From Persia came magic, pertaining to the Magi, whom the Anglo-Saxons in their version of the Bible story had translated as Wise Men; also caravan, candy, lilac, jasmine and orange. The last of these, starting as *narang*, reached France as *narange* but lost its initial 'n' there (which adhered to the article *une*) before coming on to England. And from distant eastern lands came the names of their strange wild beasts—lion, tiger, elephant and so on—embellishing travellers' tales from the earliest times.

The discovery of America at the end of the fifteenth century brought in a new era of word-borrowing for all Europe, and the exciting words brought back from across the Atlantic were passed round among the participating nations, each modifying them to its own taste. The first to arrive were from the Caribbean islands, brought by Columbus and other Spanish explorers. The word cannibal is an ignorant attempt at the name of the islanders (who were not cannibals at all), and their own words brought back at that time include hammock, canoe, tobacco, potatoes and hurricane. Shakespeare seized on the last of these using it twice while still in its Spanish form. When Lear commanded, 'You hurricanoes spout', the word was still new to England.

By this time English seamen were playing a major role in exploration and the flow of exotic words reaching Britain from across the oceans has never ceased. A high proportion of them are the names of new commodities that have added variety to our diet, or of living creatures or plants unknown before, or of buildings or cultural objects of the natives. The degree to which they have entered our language has depended largely on their usefulness to us, and on whether they have caught our imagination. Bananas from a native language of the Congo, and chocolate from Aztec, followed later by tomatoes from the same source, are now entirely familiar to us. Less likely to be seen but easy to talk of are such items as wigwams, tomahawks, igloos, llamas, and kangaroos, while even the poor dodo has supplied a useful metaphor.

But beyond these alien words now so familiar to us are thousands more that crowd the pages of the dictionary with true exotics that hardly any of us know, the words made use of by the most ruthless setters of crosswords and winners of scrabble contests, and otherwise known only by experts in some -ology or those who live in the right foreign place. In each remote land where English speakers have settled they have absorbed more of the native words than have reached the central pool of the language. Americans use more of their native Indian words than are generally known elsewhere; those who have lived in India talk of dhobies and dhotis and much more obscure matters; Australians have in their speech more aboriginal words than the very few—like boomerang—that we all know. I myself having been born in New Zealand might talk to a compatriot of the rata or the kowhai, the song of the tui or the habits of the kea, but though all these words are in the OED I would not expect anyone but a New Zealander to know them.

However, a few Polynesian words have been swept into the mainstream of English. One picked up by early explorers of the Pacific and much in vogue in England now is taboo. The common meaning of 'unmentionable' conveys but little of the deep, complicated magic that the native word tapu implies. (The stress is on the 'a', a long 'a' as in 'father'.) Its nearest translation would be 'sacred', but in English it is used as noun, verb or adjective as well as mispronounced, a sure sign of true adoption.

So many English people have lived in India, many of them coming home again to settle, that English has acquired Indian words at all stages of borrowing. The pukka sahib type of word is so exclusively Anglo-Indian that it can't be used in any other connection, but there are other more useful words that have slipped into our speech almost unnoticed and found permanent employment—cot, for instance, (Hindu khat) originally a small light bed, not necessarily for a child. How useful it is. We should be quite at a loss without it. Bungalow also has come to stay. So also pundit, the English version of Pandit, the title of a man of learning. Less pleasant but much heard now is thug, from which we have coined thuggery.

One of the best words we have taken from India is jungle.

We may know it is Indian—it is not so totally absorbed as cot—but we use it in many contexts and so expressively. When we talk of the jungle of politics it implies a confused tangle in which there is danger, ruthlessness and a fascination that leads one on. Another strong suggestive word is juggernaut. For a long time we knew it only as an obsolete Indian phenomenon, useful for metaphors, but now it has suddenly acquired a new practical application for the oversized foreign lorries that invade our roads. 'We don't want the jugs down this street,' I heard a man say, and I wondered if the abbreviation has a big future like bus and taxi. Time will show.

But it is from America that most of the additions to the vocabulary of English have come in recent times. I am not thinking of the stream of popular clichés that issue forth from the States and are taken up eagerly wherever English is spoken, particularly if they are launched in 'show business' which is one of them. I mean individual words that are positively new to English.

In its colourful history America has absorbed people of many foreign language groups besides the native Indians already mentioned—Spanish, French, Dutch, for instance, in large numbers—and has adopted words freely from all of them. This also goes for Canada, especially in regard to French. Many of the words so borrowed, such as prairie from French, ranch and canyon from Spanish, remain part of the North American scene, though known far beyond it, but others from the same source have passed into English speech anywhere. Stampede, for instance, can be used in many contexts, such as the summer sales, without a thought of cattle. Other Spanish words that we all now know include bonanza and the fashionable barbecue and patio. A few years ago we just sat 'outside' or on the terrace, or crazy-paving, but now it has to be a patio. More Spanish words have come into English speech by way of America than direct from Spain.

In the early years of their independence Americans felt much bitterness against Britain and enthusiasm for France

85

who had helped them in their fight for freedom. Everything French was fashionable and they formed the habit of adopting French words quite separately from what was going on in England, which is why they have so many Latin-based words, like apartment, elevator, eraser and faucet, corresponding to the briefer English flat, lift, rubber and tap. It didn't always work out like that. The English gave the French word, pavement, a new use as they improved their streets while the Americans coined their own word, sidewalk, out of English ingredients, but more often it was the other way round. At this time, in the early nineteenth century, the two main branches of the language were moving rapidly apart, but now that the hard feelings are gone and travelling is so much easier they seem to be coming together again to some extent. Not that people in England have much tendency to adopt those Americanisms like sidewalk and elevator that were established in the last century—or *vice versa*—these remain different and are no trouble to visitors in either direction, but words that are newly fashionable now in the States spread round the English-speaking world as fast as they are uttered.

Slang as we have noticed before is always a hotbed of new racy expressions, and America with its background of half-forgotten languages to draw on has a great facility in producing lively new oddities—new to us, that is, though they may have long histories behind them somewhere, like zombi, an African word remembered by generations of black families. At the other end of the scale, the intellectuals are always concocting new technical terms out of fragments of Latin and Greek and building them up with more and more prefixes and suffixes. Ever since the Renaissance, scholars everywhere have used these ancient languages to make an exact vocabulary for each new science, but nowhere has it been done on such a scale and with such gusto as in modern America.

The languages of the various technologies are the dialects of today, each comprehensible only to its own devotees, but not local any more, in fact world-wide. Their specialised terms if kept within the bounds of the text books, lecture rooms and wherever the experts meet hardly affect the mainstream of the language, but in America they have a way of seeping through into general conversation. In particular, the special jargon of psychology has become immensely popular and words like paranoid and ambivalent are tossed about at social gatherings with little more meaning than—jittery and doubtful. These words were not even in the OED a decade ago. Now they and others like them are heard on every side, and most of them have been launched from America.

3   Gaps in Borrowing

After so much talk of borrowing we should pause to think about what we have not borrowed when we might easily have done so, for we have been highly selective, taking large quantities here and none there according to the fashion of the time.

We have, for instance, adopted extraordinarily little from German, and when you consider that for more than a century our royal family and court were predominantly German, this fact is remarkable. It is partly due to the immense influence of France in manners, fashion and culture over the whole of Europe at that time, which affected the royal courts in German states as well as the leaders of fashion in England, but it also underlines the unpopularity of our own court during its most German period. Again, when you think of the giants of music who were German-speaking you would expect to find more of their words among musical terms. But in this art the Italians had led the way so completely in the seventeenth century that gifted musicians throughout Europe from that time onwards grew up from childhood to use their terminology.

There is a misapprehension which one sometimes hears voiced that a large part of our language 'comes from German'. This is because it is said to belong to the Germanic branch of the Indo-European language. But English is no more descended from German than *vice versa*; they are equal descendants with other northern tongues of the same prehistoric ancestor. The confusion arises from our use of the word German for this particular modern language and the people who speak it. They don't use it themselves; it is our peculiarity to apply it to them. They call themselves *Deutsch* (which we use for the race we ought to call Netherlanders); the French call them *Allemands* and the Italians *Tedesci*. And the fact remains that since our ancestors parted company with theirs somewhere in northern Europe at least fifteen hundred years ago we have had little verbal influence on each other. Modern English has far closer affinities with French than with German, and when we say that all the deeper roots of our vocabulary are Germanic we are using this term only in its wider sense.

It is quite hard to find any German words that we have fully adopted. There is waltz, one of the few popular musical terms created in Germany, but the dance itself has gone out of fashion; there are knapsack and rucksack, both from Germany, and kindergarten, but that has almost disappeared in favour of nursery school. Blitzkrieg, shortened to blitz, was much used just after the second world war, both for the real thing and metaphorically ('I'm having a blitz on the sitting-room', that is, cleaning it up), but it is fading fast now. We have taken far more from our nearer neighbours, the Dutch.

But nearness is not what promotes borrowing, not half so much as admiration and fashion. For the most striking omission among languages from which the English might easily have borrowed is its closest neighbour of all, Welsh. Apart from place-names (which are of great significance) we have imported practically nothing from this source right on our doorstep. When the English first invaded Britain and forced their way across it, the language they encountered all the way was an old form of Welsh, and even in the late Saxon period there must still have been as much Welsh as English spoken in this island (bearing in mind that Cornish and Cumbrian were branches of Welsh). Now the tide has receded so far that the proportion here in Britain is over a hundred to one in favour of English, and in the world at large, where English-speakers are counted in hundreds of millions, Welsh is almost unknown. But it is still a living language and receiving better treatment now than it did a hundred years ago when Welsh children were punished for speaking it in their own schools.

One of the reasons why the English have taken so few words from Welsh is that in the early period of contact the oncoming English had little tendency to pick up foreign

89

words at all—except such place-names as they found ready-made for them. As previously mentioned, the coming of Christianity impressed some Latin on them, and later the Norman Conquest enforced much French; after that it was always to Europe that they looked for culture and advancement. Then came the glamour of exotic words from far away. We know and use far more words from India or South America than we do from the other language in our own island.

But perhaps the strongest reason why this is so is that Welsh is so totally unlike English that there is no meeting point between them. When Danes settled in northern England their language was so similar to that of the Angles of Northumbria that Danish words could easily slip into English sentences. But not so between English and Britons (or Welsh as the English called them), only total uncomprehension which the English made no attempt to overcome. It has been left to the Welsh, who are natural linguists, to learn English as required, and this they have done to good effect producing orators, actors, poets and other writers in English, while their literature remains closed to us. Our excuse must be (besides our linguistic laziness) that Welsh is an extremely difficult language for anyone not born to it.

The Celtic languages—once spoken all across central Europe but now surviving only as Welsh, Gaelic and Breton—belong like the Germanic tongues to the Indo-European family, but branched off from the main trunk in prehistoric times, developing their own idiosyncrasies which are like those of no other language. In particular the habit of changing the first letters of words according to regular grammatical rules is too much for most would-be learners. When you find that a simple noun like the word for bread can be *fara*, *mara* or *bara* in different circumstances and have inflexional endings too, you are inclined to give up.

We all know a few Welsh words—corgi, cromlech—but hardly more than can be counted on the fingers of one hand.

The only one as far as I know that has been totally accepted as if it were our own is Dad or Daddy. The original word is *tad* but it regularly changes to *dad* in many word groups. An English visitor in a Welsh church may be surprised to hear the priest invoke God as 'Dad', but it is the regular word for father, formal or informal. It may have been among Welsh and English children playing together that it passed into English, its passage helped by the fact that it is such a simple sound, easy for a child to make. It is first recorded in colloquial English as early as 1500, but it took a long time to climb the social ladder and find acceptance in all classes. By 1900 it had fully arrived, completely ousting Papa which had been the standard way for well-brought-up children to address their fathers for over a century. In America this has survived strongly in the form of Pop or Poppa, but Daddy is used there too. Strangely enough another Welsh word of the same sort is following in the wake of Dad, for in recent years English children have taken to calling their grandmothers Nan, and that is Welsh too.

Other Celtic words have come into English from the Gaelic of Ireland and of the Scottish Highlands, which is virtually the same language. From Ireland come shamrock, bog, banshee and bard. But the Celtic languages are so closely linked and their early culture so similar that bard could equally well have come from Welsh. We have rather taken to this word, applying it in mock romantic style to Shakespeare, and coining from it bardolatry to describe the goings on at Stratford.

From Scottish Gaelic (fast fading now) come a few more Celtic words, and here the situation is different, for the basic language of the Lowlands is a northern form of English, as long established there as it is in England. It incorporates a good many Gaelic words as well as Norse ones from Viking invaders and so forms a bridge between Gaelic and English, a halfway-house that is totally lacking between English and Welsh. This Lowland Scots language has produced great writers whose works can be understood by English speakers anywhere—or nearly so. (How many have sung Auld Lang Syne without the least idea of half its meaning?) Sir Walter Scott, out of fashion now but vastly admired for over a century, was one of the first to publicise Scotland and ever since his time we have all known such words as glen, loch, brae, plaid, sporran and claymore, though we use them only in a Scottish context. The Gaelic word best known to all the world is whisky (literally water, short for *uisge beatha*, water of life), while of the few Gaelic words that have passed right into English use so that their origins are forgotten the most widely used is probably trousers, but of this we can think further when we come to the subject of clothes.

On the whole the Celtic tongues, once spoken along the whole western frontier of the English people from Cornwall to Scotland, have had only a minimal influence on the English language compared with the flood of French, Latin and ancient Greek that poured in from the other direction.

4   How Much Borrowing?

When one has thought about borrowed words as much as I have, one begins to feel that English must be more than half made up of them, and the *Encyclopedia Britannica* in its article on the language says, 'The vocabulary of modern English is roughly half Germanic (Old English and Scandinavian) and half Romance (French and Latin) with copious importations from elsewhere.' But I can't agree unreservedly with that. It all depends on what you mean by vocabulary. If you were taking the proportions of the dictionary in which all words from the most familiar to the most exotic are given on an equal footing, then there would be more loan-words. But no human being ever spoke in such proportions. Everyone uses some rare words but far more common ones. If you mean the normal vocabulary of speech and writing— whether good or bad, learned or ignorant—then at least three-quarters of it is still Anglo-Saxon.

I wrote that paragraph just as it came to me with no particular plan in mind but now I see that it will serve as a specimen of very ordinary English. It contains 159 words and 29 of them are of foreign origin which makes a percentage of 18. And when I say 18 per cent, I am speaking in numbers not in bulk, for borrowed words are generally much longer than our home-grown products. As the paragraph is on an academic subject this percentage is fairly high though well under a quarter. I have counted it all including repetitions because my object is to see what proportion of the whole is borrowed, and words that are often repeated are generally those that are the most important either to the structure of the language or to the matter on hand. There might be a case for omitting 'the' and 'a' as insignificant, but if one starts omitting, the passage is no longer complete in its natural form. I am not trying to make a judgement on our speech, just looking at it to see what it is made of.

But it would be foolish to judge by such a scrap. So let

us look further, and why not at the very best. Shakespeare for a start. Suppose we plunge right into *Macbeth*.

> Is this a dagger that I see before me
> Its handle towards my hand? Come let me clutch thee.
> I have thee not and yet I see thee still.

Pure English. But soon we shall have 'fatal vision', 'false creation' and 'Tarquin's ravishing strides'. The whole speech down to 'The bell invites me' is just 200 words and contains 32 loan-words, or 16 per cent.

You might think that *Macbeth* with its primitive background would be less likely to contain sophisticated words than some of the other plays, so let us try Hamlet at his most philosophical.

> To be or not to be, that is the question.
> Whether 'tis nobler in the mind to suffer
> The slings and arrows of outrageous fortune—

Question, noble, suffer and fortune are all of course French, but slings and arrows splendidly English. Outrageous is half and half. The whole speech down to his seeing Ophelia (260 words) contains only 39 foreigners, all French or Latin. That is just 15 per cent.

Now a sonnet. I tried, 'Shall I compare thee to a summer's day?', and found in 114 words only 14 loan-words or 13 per cent. And finally for something much lighter I turned to a comedy and took a bit of Puck—pure fun and poetry—

> Now the hungry lion roars
> And the wolf behowls the moon,
> While the heavy ploughman snores,
> All with weary task foredone—

And so on to the end of the speech, 112 words and only eight of them of foreign origin, starting with lion and task. From these and other tests I calculate that Shakespeare used on average only about 14 per cent of borrowed words, and less in his lyrics than in more serious speeches.

We think of Milton as the most classical of our poets but though his work is scattered with names from Greek mythology, its basic language is as English as Shakespeare's—or very nearly so. His deeply-felt sonnet on his blindness contains only 17 foreign-based words out of 114, and—to take a different type of poem—the opening passage of *Lycidas*, which is almost the same length, has only 14 loan-words, three of them being the name Lycidas, lovingly repeated. Like all the best English poets, Milton excelled in the mingling of native and exotic words with magical results:

> Sabrina fair, listen where thou art sitting
> Under the glassy, cool, translucent wave—

or in more sombre mood:

> Dark, dark, dark, irrecoverably dark.

The long Latin 'translucent' and 'irrecoverably', contrasting so strongly with the English 'cool' and 'dark', serve in each case to intensify the effect. Shakespeare was always doing it— multitudinous seas—quintessence of dust—and in our own time we see it in Eliot's description of midwinter days as 'sempiternal' and, in the same line, 'sodden'.

Most modern poets prefer to use English words, though they will turn anywhere for the one they want. Here is Dylan Thomas, pouring them out in spontaneous profusion:

Now as I was young and easy under the apple boughs
About the lilting house and happy as the grass was green,
    The night above the dingle starry,
    Time let me hail and climb
    Golden in the heydays of his eyes,
And honoured among the wagons, I was prince of the apple towns
And once below a time I lordly had the trees and leaves
    Trail with daisies and barley
    Down the rivers of the windfall light.

And as I was green and carefree, famous among the barns
About the happy yard, and singing as the farm was home—

I shall stop there—though it would be pleasant to continue—for we have had a hundred words, enough to count the score. Only seven borrowed words and all of them adopted so long ago that you would never feel they were foreigners: easy, honoured, prince, trail, rivers, famous and farm. You might wonder at farm being borrowed when it seems so English but it was what the Normans called the Saxon homesteads (OF *ferme*) because they had to pay a firm or regular rent. Contrariwise you might think wagon was French because of the *wagons lits* on the Continent, but that is a case of the French borrowing from us. The traffic has gone both ways.

The poems of Dylan Thomas, earthy and elemental, show a low proportion of imported words, but even the academic T. S. Eliot averages only about 14 per cent, and many poets of this century use far less. In the extract from the poem by Edward Thomas that ends this book, just nine words out of 106 have come from alien roots. In Hardy's poems it is easy to find whole verses of pure English origin, but seldom whole poems because so many early borrowings have become like natives.

Next we must try some modern prose but it is hard to know what to select. Literature offers an impossibly wide choice and, lest I should be accused of picking something likely to prove my point, I will take some *Times* leaders. They are at least well-written and not unduly pompous, but as they deal chiefly with politics, economics and international affairs, they are liable to contain more importations than are found in less serious writing. I have now taken passages of a hundred words each from five of them—taken at random except that I avoided paragraphs with a lot of proper names—and the result averages out at 30 per cent of loan-words. I call that high.

After that heavy diet I need an antidote and turn happily to P. G. Wodehouse. Five passages of the same length as those from the *Times*—bits of narrative without dialogue—bring me back to a comfortable 13 per cent and provide the necessary relaxation. It is not that his vocabulary is limited—far from it—but it is essentially human and not weighted down with all those -isations and -atives and -istics that seem so essential to politics.

Our politicians when they speak use fewer of these Latinisms than they do in writing, and in general those who are highest in government circles speak plainer English than those in lesser positions, presumably because plain speaking goes with clear thinking and the clear thinkers rise to the top, or so one hopes. When I listen to political speakers I am struck with the resilience of our old vernacular in the face of all the foreign competition and how not only all those little words that hold it together but also a lot of vigorous Anglo-Saxon compounds, old and new, are heard on all sides: breakthrough (very much in fashion), backlash, stopgap, stranglehold, shortcomings (but never longcomings).

The worst offenders in preferring borrowed words to English, the borrowed ones being in general more formal, are to be found in the lower ranks of officialdom where a little authority gives a sense of importance and a wish to be correct and dignified, and it is specially so in written reports. I read in a local parish magazine that someone in spite of poor health 'would continue to operate in his employment situation'. But the well-meaning writer would not, I think, ever have spoken those words. To a group of friends, or even strangers, he would have said, 'He's going to keep his job.'

It is often said that most officials—especially in government offices—will never use one word where they can use three, but my complaint is often just the reverse, that they prefer one long word to three short ones. It is in the nature of English that many verbs are made of a combination of short words for which the French or Latin equivalent is one long one. For 'come in' the imported synonym is 'enter'; for 'go on', continue; for 'set up', establish; 'do away with', abolish; 'think over', consider; 'get ready', prepare; 'put up with', tolerate: and so on, almost indefinitely. In such cases the

97

official will always choose the loan-word as if he were nervous of the short words and certainly he wouldn't care to put them in writing. He would rather hospitalise a man than send him to hospital, and would prefer a progressive dialogue to talking things over.

But however much the classical-based concoctions are loaded onto a sentence, there still remains its solid English framework which is more than half of what we say.

To prove this to my own satisfaction I decided to do one more test, this time of the most ordinary and spontaneous speech I could find to counteract the literary items I had taken before. I gathered my material from radio and television using unscripted discussions and impromptu interviews with anyone from experts on any subject to casual bystanders. I wrote it down just as it came with no editing, but never more than two or three sentences from one person so as to bring in the maximum number of speakers and topics, and as I found it rather amusing I went on until I had amassed four thousand words spoken by nearly a hundred individuals.

In this hotch-potch of talk I found the proportion of loan-words was fifteen per cent, about the same as I found in Shakespeare but only half of what you might expect in a *Times* leader. I also found that of all the words we have borrowed, the one we use most is 'very'. This was adopted early in Middle English from the Old French *verai* (true) which in Modern French has become *vrai*. We have used it so much that it has drifted into an adverbial use that can intensify anything. (The Old English word that it replaced was *swithe*, pronounced 'swithy', a total victory here for the foreigner.)

I also found that I was quite justified in saying that the basis of our speech is purely English. Much though we use 'very', there are literally dozens of other words, all short and simple, that we use far more, and they are all English. These can be seen on page 142.

VI

THE PEOPLE'S CHOICE

1 Fashions in Words

I often wonder why some words after centuries of steady use should fail and disappear for no apparent reason. It isn't old age, for words can outlive anything as poets have often pointed out. It can only be fashion, whose vagaries are un-accountable.

Medieval peasants used to swink in the fields. Swink and sweat went conveniently together in the alliteration that came naturally to English poets. It was a synonym for work, both time-honoured words; but when toil and labour came to join them it was apparently one too many and swink was the one to go.

Then why should steed, once an ordinary word for a large strong horse, have become quite unusable except in mock-heroic style? Did the romantic poets make it too romantic? And there was that neat little pair don and doff, which were contractions of do on and do off, and entirely practical; why should they have to give way to put on and take off, which are in no way better?

It seems we must have change. All are agreed on that. Even the stuffiest of us who are always complaining about the mis-use or mispronunciation of individual words know in our hearts that the language can't stand still. We only hope to steady its course a little, so that it doesn't suffer too much damage and lose its best qualities.

Naturally the young are more inclined to novelty than their elders and it is in their speech, as it always was, that most of the verbal changes originate. But listening critically to their talk I hear hardly any new words. It is all a matter of using old words in a new way and then copying each other, for much as they wish to speak differently from their parents, they want even more to speak like their friends of their own age. A new usage used to take time to spread, but now a pop star can flash it across the world in hours.

When I was a student I lived in digs (short, I believe, for diggings from miners' slang). But why? Now they have a pad (an old word used in thieves' cant for anything soft to sleep on). Why again? They wear gear and express admiration by saying a person is cool or neat, but these epithets have no relation to temperature or tidiness, which is indeed the last virtue that they seem to value. Square, formerly used in praise ('Fair and square'), is now derogatory. No new words here, only new uses.

Such fashions may be very short-lived but sometimes the new usage—however illogical—has a permanent effect. The young may go on using the same expression as they grow older until it becomes general. It is this sort of thing that may account for the odd changes of meaning that have affected some words in the past. Caught up on a wave of fashion a word can lose its original character, and when it is dropped again, survive only in some quite new capacity from that in which it started out.

Take, for example, pretty. In Old English it meant cunning, crafty and astute. Then from about 1450 onwards it suddenly appears very frequently with a wide range of meanings, all of lively approbation, like super, fine or delightful of the present day. This praise was not at first concerned with looks or with women, in fact it was more often applied to men, 'a pretty fellow' being a big, strong, resourceful man, and probably a bit of a wag. 'A pretty fortune' was a large one and that idea is still with us when we say 'It cost a pretty penny.' Shakespeare used it in a more modern way for women (Whither faring, pretty sweeting?) but perhaps with more idea of lively charm than of looks. It was not till the early nineteenth century that it really settled down into its present meaning.

By way of comparison we may note the career of 'acute' in America. Applied to a person, 'acute' means much what 'pretty' did originally. In the States it was shortened in popular speech to cute, and look what that means now.

Another adjective that has had its nature changed out of all recognition by the whims of fashion is 'nice'. Most people know that it once meant exact, precise and fastidious, but that is not the beginning of its story. When first it came into England in the Middle English period it meant stupid, being derived from the Latin *nescius*—ignorant. It seems that its stupidity consisted chiefly in being hard to please, over-fussy and pernickety, but gradually this improved into being selective and meticulous in a more reasonable way. In the late eighteenth century when refined and delicate manners were much admired in high society, it was fashionable to be nice, and from then on it became a general commendation that grew vaguer and vaguer as the years rolled by.

But though nice has for some time been used to excess, it has never signified ecstatic favour—never been in the same class with stunning, ripping, topping, divine, heavenly, marvellous, smashing, super, terrific and others that have followed each other as peaks of adulation in this century. And therein lies the secret of its success. Nice has always retained a character of moderation such as Lord Chesterfield would have approved. The young have always liked to make their praise as strong as possible, building up their favourite adjectives with intensifying adverbs—awfully jolly, absolutely gorgeous—but the slightly older and more staid, a numerous class, are content with 'very nice', which saves them trouble as it will do for anything at all and requires no thought.

We all agree that 'nice' is overworked but we go on using it. In our love of understatement and dread of sounding pompous, we are often glad to fall back on it in preference to something stronger, and with the right tone of voice can make it mean just what we want. 'I think that's rather nice', can be decided praise; while 'Actually he's a very nice

101

person', is high commendation, implying the major virtues of kindness and reliability. No other word can convey this so well, in a way that is light and easy.

Some adjectives stand up to a vast amount of hard use without ever suffering these strange twists of meaning. Such a one is 'lovely' which has carried the theme of gentleness and beauty for over a thousand years. It is taking a great beating at the present time, used almost as much as O.K. (Tomorrow suit you? Two o'clock? Lovely.) And yet we can still speak of a lovely garden or piece of music in a way that gives it the old value. It is a lovely word, and long may it escape destruction.

'Fair' in its old sense of beautiful is never heard now except in well-known quotations, such as 'My fair lady'. But it still survives strongly in other subsidiary meanings such as blonde (because that colouring was once the most admired), equitable, and—a sad fall from grace—middling. (When someone's condition is described as fair it is pretty poor.) The original meaning was ousted by 'beautiful' which came in as a fashionable new hybrid in the Tudor period. Neither Shakespeare nor Milton used it much, each greatly preferring fair to describe all kinds of beauty, but the new word evidently took the public fancy and has remained in favour.

Of course it is not only the young who like to use the latest in-word. While they are describing their idols as smashing, great, fab or cosmic, their parents and the more discriminating of the younger set are also groping for words of praise that are at once apt and fashionable, but their choices of— splendid, brilliant, dazzling, tremendous, fantastic and so on will each in turn be slightly dimmed by over-use and need replacement. Sophisticated, which until recently meant false and deceitful, is now being used as praise. New gadgets and equipment are called sophisticated meaning that they are complicated and ultra-modern, and some people like to be thought so too.

A theme that has regularly supplied words of praise (and

the choice must betray something in our nature) is magic. Charming, entrancing and enchanting are all based on it; so also marvellous which has been used so much that some of its magic has faded; while among the teenagers wizard had a great run. Another of this group, though you might not think it, is glamorous which was all the rage in the great days of Hollywood. Glamour was a Scottish dialect form of 'grammar' or 'grammarye', which itself was an old word for enchantment. (Grammar means the study of words, and words have always been at the heart of magic.) The change from 'r' to 'l' may have come about through association with all those gleaming, glittering words that I spoke of earlier, and adds a sparkle to the meaning. It was Sir Walter Scott who brought this half-forgotten old word into use again and then a century passed before journalists took it up. For a time glamorous rode the crest of the wave, but it is in decline now and what star performers need today is charisma.

There are other subjects besides praise that are always calling for new epithets. A tendency to exaggerate seems natural to the human race and ever since the cavemen started telling their families about the mammoths they had nearly captured people have been finding new words to stress size. The oldest we have is great, which is now used so much for general commendation that its first meaning is nearly lost. In support of that came big and huge (both of uncertain origin) and then large, vast, enormous, monstrous, prodigious, gigantic, colossal, stupendous, astronomical, mammoth, jumbo and the all-purpose super. Commercial advertisers vie with each other in this field, always seeking for something new, but since all their words are so superlative it is only by looking at the articles in question that you can discover whether the monster pack, the maxi carton or the new jumbo size is the larger. It could be that the economy offer will exceed them all.

But the theme that has caused the severest wear and tear on adjectives is that which describes alarming or distressing

103

circumstances, or often occasions that are no worse than embarrassing. Awful and terrible, once powerful words, have been so weakened that their adverbial forms are now the mildest of qualifiers (it was awfully kind of you, terribly sweet). Others now going down the same path, are frightful, dreadful and horrible, the last of these having been tried in several variations such as horrific and horrendous. Ghastly (the Scottish form of ghostly) was much in vogue for a time, but has since given way to traumatic.

On the whole when a new word takes over, the old ones remain, weakened but still in use, so that the total stock increases all the time. But some that start only as slang and never rise above that class can disappear completely. 'Did you really say ripping when you were young?' my granddaughter asked me, rather like asking if I ever wore a bustle. Of course I did and it was no sillier than smashing which some of her contemporaries are still saying. Or was it? I suppose smashing reflects the idea of a smash hit, bang on. I can't find any idea to account for ripping but once I thought that to have a ripping time was absolute bliss.

2   Fashions in Clothes

No subject is more open to the vagaries of fashion and therefore to a continual coming and going of words than that of clothes. New garments bring new names which flourish for a while but may soon disappear again and be quite forgotten—houpelandes, liripipes, wimples, henins, pickadills, galligaskins, farthingales, stomachers, lappets, frontlets, tippets, crinolines, pelisses—where are they now? But it is never safe to say that a word is gone, especially in the world of fashion, for dress designers and promoters, seeking a new name, can revive an old one instead. The medieval jerkin has staged a return recently and so has the Victorian pinafore, though in name only for the new adult dress bears little resemblance to the child's frilly apron. And even jeans that seem so modern take their name from a material made in Genoa that was known in England as *geane* before 1500.

Some names go and some show great staying power even when the garments themselves keep changing. Coat, for instance, has named many different items of our clothing since Norman times, and a very English word it has become in spite of having come to us from France, for it was never much used there and not at all in the way we use it now. We see it first as a *cote de maille*, a leather body-covering with metal rings sewn on to it for protection, and then as a loose strip of cloth worn over the mail and embroidered with the knight's heraldic device—hence a coat of arms. From that it developed into a long sleeveless tunic called a *surcote* worn by either sex over more fitted garments, for Norman castles were cold and many layers of cloth advisable. Then came the short tight-fitting tunic called a *cotehardie* (or just *cote*), so short that some thought it shocking. Several of Chaucer's company wore a 'cote' and hood. Hood has never changed, but 'cote' soon went out again in favour of jerkin and after that doublet (so called because it was made of double material); this was the principal upper garment for men for over a century.

Meanwhile 'coats' could also signify the long clothes worn by babies or the 'short coats' to which they were promoted as little children, or women's underskirts, which seem to have been *petti*coats only in the sense that they were less important than the gowns that went over them, or even the furry skins of animals—a truly versatile word.

It was not until the reign of Charles II that a total change of fashion brought in the coat as we know it, that is an outer garment with sleeves and a front opening that can be buttoned up or not. Ever since then it has kept this general character and the word for it has remained so steady that it seems unlikely ever to change. But who can tell?

I have mentioned elsewhere how we took the word 'dress' from French and used it for clothing, a subject with which it has no connection in France, and how we did something similar with 'suit' which should mean a set of things which follow each other. When Hamlet speaks of 'customary suits of solemn black', Shakespeare is thinking as we would of outfits of matching items; but what about a child's play-suit or a space-suit which are both essentially one-piece? Once we get hold of a word there is no controlling what we will do with it.

The evidence as to what the Anglo-Saxons called their clothes is somewhat scanty, but some of the words that they used for essential garments (with modifications of sound and spelling) have run the whole course from King Alfred's day to our own, including shirt, breeches, hat, hood and shoes. The shirt (of which something was said on page 35) has had a largely masculine character in its long career, and women have used other names for their version of it, English 'shift', and later French 'chemise' or 'blouse', but now we can all wear shirts.

Breeches have had some ups and downs—and that could be taken literally—but the word has always survived. At first as OE *brēc*, the plural of *brōc* (like tooth and teeth), it was used for those loose leg-coverings bound around with thongs that were worn by Saxons and Vikings alike. In the later Middle Ages when they were cut to fit more closely, reaching elegantly from waist to foot, they were more often called hose, especially by the fashionable, but the workers in the fields covered their legs as most convenient, and this meant the old-style breeches with separate wrappings for the lower legs and feet which they called stocks or stockings. Just how stock took on this meaning isn't clear; it is one of those basic Old English words that were used in many ways at an early date. While loan-words from France generally came in at a high social level and descended slowly to the people, colloquial home-grown words began at the bottom and rose upwards. This is what 'stockings' did, reaching the court in Tudor times, when even at the height of the 'doublet and hose' fashion Ophelia could complain of the untidy state of Hamlet's 'stockings'.

As soon as the extremely brief 'trunk hose' of the Elizabethans began to descend once more down the thigh they were called breeches again (the old plural form having now acquired the usual -es). By the reign of Charles I they had reached a point just below the knee where they remained for nearly two centuries. Below them were stockings; the word hose was out and has never really recovered, except for modern use in the garden, though shopkeepers have tried ineffectively to keep it going.

It was a great event in the sartorial world when in about 1800 the elegant knee-breeches that had been in fashion so long began to move again, descending in a few years to the ankles. The same thing had happened in Paris—as a symbol of the general breaking with convention—and there the new garments were called in a slightly jocular way *pantalons*, taking the name of a figure of fun in Italian comedy, a foolish old man whose nether garments hung down to his feet. This name can be taken a stage further back to St Pantaleon, an

107

obscure Roman martyr of the third century whose connection with the comedy lay in nothing but his name. Meanwhile the new long 'pantaloons' were all the rage among the young bucks of Regency London, though frowned on by many who thought them too sloppy and casual for decent society. A new name was urgently needed, for 'pantaloons' seemed too comic, slops, as some called them, was inelegant, and as the whole subject was considered delicate, they were also referred to as unmentionables and inexpressibles.

The problem was solved from an unlikely quarter, Gaelic. The wars with France had brought Highland regiments into England and though kilts caused the most interest some Highlanders wore tartan trews (Gaelic *triubhas*) that were not unlike the new pantaloons. Anglo-Irish families also knew the word and now it was seized upon—in a slightly lengthened form as trousers—to fill the gap in England, with lasting success.

But we hadn't heard the last of 'pantaloons'. Abbreviated colloquially to pants, it came into use for men's underwear, to replace 'drawers', and also developed a feminine form, 'pantalettes', for the long frilly drawers that could be seen beneath a crinoline; and now we still have 'panties', however fleetingly (for in this department changes come very fast). But more importantly pantaloons crossed to America where, shortened again to pants, they competed more successfully against trousers than they had in England. Now today in the whole English-speaking world, pants and trousers must be fairly equally matched. St Pantaleon, who probably had no pants at all, would be much surprised. But breeches are still flourishing too for those who ride.

In the past most of the names of new fashions came from France, but there were always some from further afield. The shawl, for instance, came from Persia as early as 1662 but was not really popular until the nineteenth century when it was so greatly in favour that it is unlikely ever to be forgotten. Now new types of clothing complete with their foreign names can come from anywhere: anoraks from the Eskimos, ponchos from South America, while bikinis take their name from a tiny coral island in the Pacific.

Apart from our own home-grown wool and linen, the names of materials have generally come from far away. Silk was known to the Saxons, who called it *sioloc*, but the word had passed through so many languages on its way from the Far East that its exact origin is unclear. Damask came from Damascus, muslin from Mosul in Iraq, calico from Calicut in India, denim from Nîmes in France (de Nîmes), and so on. In contrast to these the names of modern synthetic materials are as artificial as the stuffs themselves. Rayon (1924) and nylon (1938) were made up with the same ending as cotton to simulate a natural sound. Terylene (1951) is a contraction of terephthalic-ethylene, but as the scientists keep on devising new materials these invented words follow each other too fast to attain real permanence in the language.

Of course the general public produces its own names too for what it wears, as it always has, and it is the people's voice that counts. It is they who have coined such natural words as shorts; and also tights which began in theatrical slang and has long been waiting in the wings to make a more official entry, as it has now done. But popular coinages are not always happy. Some years ago the woollen upper garment that was pleasantly named from the island of Jersey whose fishermen wore it, became unaccountably a jumper (another nautical term), and then a pullover, which ultra-English expression was taken up in France and is still to be heard in several European countries. Then all these were overtaken by the unattractive 'sweater'. This change reflects the adulation of sport for it was among those who took violent exercise, particularly rowing men at the universities, that it originated. It was popularised in America (where the jumper has become a pinafore dress) and bounced back more fashionable than before, but I find its continued success surprising in an age that is so strongly anti-sweat, judging by the sales of

109

deodorants whose advertisements are couched in much more restrained language than the popularity of 'sweater' would suggest. But we may have another change soon.

One more garment that owes its name to university sportsmen is the blazer. In the late nineteenth century men's clothes in England were extremely sombre in hue (excepting only for soldiers and huntsmen) but at the universities sports jackets began to show the College colours, at first with restraint. When members of the Lady Margaret Boat Club at Cambridge appeared in scarlet jackets it created a sensation. It is said that horses shied at them and they were dubbed blazers from their blazing colour. Now they are worn by anyone and need no longer be bright.

Like sweater, this name is formed from an Old English word. The earliest known meaning of blaze is a torch.

3 Naming Inventions

Language, like nature, abhors a vacuum. As soon as a new concept is formed in the mind it needs a word to express it, and a word will be found. It may not be ideal and a better one may supersede it, but the new idea must have some name from the start.

Inventors like to make names for their own creations, their usual practice being to put together particles from Greek or Latin, and in this way many inventions have been successfully named with words like telephone, photograph, microscope, that have passed easily into the language. Within the specialised departments of science much more formidable conglomerations of syllables are put together with results that are more like formulas than words, but any invention that is going to be used widely by the public must have a name that they will take to. If they don't like the official name they won't use it and will call the new product something else. If Alexander Graham Bell hadn't produced a good, usable word like 'telephone' without delay we would now be calling it a ringer or a speaker or some other such easy name of our own choice.

The pioneers of the railway, knowing that the great significance of the new machines lay in their ability to move from place to place, called them 'locomotive engines' or just 'locomotives'. But what most impressed the onlookers was that these amazing things could drag a whole 'train' of carriages behind them. Train was already an old word, descended remotely from the Latin *trahir*, to drag, and it had been used in England for centuries for anything that trailed behind, like the procession of servants and baggage carts that followed a nobleman when he moved about, or the long robes of a royal gown that dragged on the ground unless carried by a page. It could also mean the following of eager students that attended a popular teacher, who would then instruct or 'train' them, and himself become their trainer; but this is taking us off on quite another tack. In fact train was a common word, which the public applied to the new machines in a comprehensive way, engines, carriages and all.

The other striking thing about these trains was that rails had to be laid for them to run on all across the country, giving rise to much discussion. As a result the standard words for this form of travel are trains and railway, the people's choice. Experts still talk of locomotives, but they are a small minority.

The early developments of the motor car were so long drawn out in several countries, that the establishment of a general name for it was for many years quite unpredictable. In England people talked of horseless carriages, a negative expression unlikely to have much future (and yet when you think how long we went on speaking of 'the wireless', which is comparable to 'horseless', you realise that nothing in language is impossible). In France the word *automobile* (self-moving) was coined on regular classical lines, and this name was given official sanction in England by the formation of the Royal Automobile Club in 1897 and the Automobile Association in 1905. But the English didn't take to it. In 1895 the expression 'motor-car' had been put forward in the *Daily Chronicle*, and they liked that much better.

The use of 'car' in this context was decidedly high-flown, for it was then a little-known word and one whose associations were fanciful rather than practical. Like the regular words for vehicles of that time, cart and carriage, and the historical chariot, it was derived from the Latin *carrus*, the wheeled vehicle of ancient Rome, but compared with the others it hardly existed except in poetry where it had sometimes taken the place of chariot if the rhythm required a single syllable. It was mostly gods or goddesses—especially Phoebus—who travelled in cars, golden affairs of uncertain shape. But early motorists, sitting up high as if enthroned and gliding forward as if by magic, must have had a godlike feeling.

Fanciful or not the English public liked the sound of 'motor car' and that is what they mostly called the strange vehicles that were appearing on the roads at the turn of the century. But as the new phenomena became more common, people were less inclined to say the double name, the only question being which of the two words would prevail. At first it seemed to be motor (as in the Motor Show). 'May I take you for a spin in my motor?' the eager suitor of that time would ask. But who would say those words now? 'Car' fought back strongly and gained the victory, so much so that in the United States, where 'automobile' had been firmly established, young Americans are now talking of their 'cars', and this word is making headway across Europe. Motor has left a substantial legacy of derived words, such as motorist, motoring and the more recent motorway, but used alone it is reverting to its earlier meaning of a mechanical device for moving anything.

Other names for modern vehicles have arrived in equally chancy ways dependent chiefly on the whims of the public. The horsedrawn vehicles used for paying passengers in cities were first called *voitures omnibus* (carriages for all) in Paris in 1828. The second part of this phrase came on to London and was quickly shortened in Cockney slang to its last syllable, which remained unchanged when the vehicles were motorised. For many decades the abbreviation was considered a vulgarism and official announcements referred to omnibuses. Today bus is not only respectable but world wide. The notice 'Buzz stop' may be seen in Crete, and in America to bus or not to bus (children to particular schools) is a burning political problem. And yet this important word is made of the merest fragment of a Latin one, only a part of its final inflexion.

In something of the same style the French *cabriolet* was popularised as cab. And then when a device was invented for measuring the distance travelled and the amount due it became a taximeter cab. The change to motorisation hardly affected the name which was in any case soon shortened again. Taxi, first recorded in 1907, was at first a very slangy expression, but what a good, distinctive, usable word it has proved—and international, too. It seems that an excellent method of getting an original word is for the inventor first to have his say and then for the public to get to work on it.

But sometimes they reject what they are offered out of hand. When large motorised cars were first introduced for taking numbers of people long distances, they were officially called charabancs—French again, but hardly used by the French who preferred *autobus*. The English people tried it out, shortened it to 'chara', didn't like it, and instead called up from the past the old-fashioned 'coach'. The coachman's whip and horn, the teams of galloping horses, the outside passengers perched on top, all these had vanished from our roads, but the word coach is back again because people liked it.

The expansion of motoring brought a whole range of attendant words, many to become international. Among those adopted most widely is the new verb to park. We are so used to it we take it for granted; but why should 'park' mean to put your car in a proper place, and mean it so obviously that all the world should use it? A park has long been a place reserved for grass and trees, perhaps with flowers, perhaps sporting facilities, but no more suited than anywhere else for leaving cars. It seems that this usage originated in the army long before cars were invented, for a place where cannons, waggons and other heavy supplies could be left when not in use. It must have begun in one particular place which happened to be called 'the park' before being put to this use, and from there it spread in army language. But the reason for its sudden extension to all drivers everywhere was the emergence of a new problem that made a verbal gap which must be filled. In the early days of motoring you just left your car wherever you liked, but as soon as that changed a special word was wanted and was found.

114

In this case the same word suited England and America, but in many of the details connected with driving we have each gone our own way—but ways that are closely parallel in spirit. In England the front of the car is the bonnet and the back part the boot. Americans call them the hood (headgear again) and the trunk, and think our words very funny. On English roads we have roundabouts and move in traffic lanes. Americans have rotaries and streams. Note how in both countries we use old familiar words for these modern arrangements. 'Lane' is certainly a bit old-world and carriage-way absurd; but then the Americans call their big toll roads turnpikes which in Britain belong to a bygone age.

Men dreamed of air travel long before there was any real prospect of it and what they spoke of was 'flying machines'. Then when flights were actually being attempted all sorts of names arose. I have before me a book on 'Modern Inventions' published in 1905 in which one chapter begins, 'Flying machines, or, as they should correctly be called, aeromobiles—'; that was one that never got off the ground. The essential feature of most early models was the thin, flat surface that was to float on the air, the plane in fact. There were biplanes, monoplanes, airplanes (in America) and aeroplanes, the last of these becoming the general favourite. Now they are often talked of just as planes. But another word now much used is aircraft, which takes its second element from the language of the sea. It has the important advantage of including more different types of machine than plane could reasonably do.

As for space travel, it is wonderful how our old language has risen to the challenge and provided most of the vocabulary for this extraordinary development. Here again we have craft, spacecraft this time, a new compound that shows the versatility of our oldest words. Craft in Old English meant skill and wisdom. In Middle English it was applied to particular skills and so to special trades. Among seamen it was skill in handling boats, and then by one of those curious side-steps

115

that words sometimes make it was the boats themselves. Now it has soared into the sky and even further.

It is too soon to know which enduring new words will come from man's exploits in outer space. Astronaut seems assured, but airmen were called aeronauts for a time and that didn't last. Perhaps they will just be spacemen and space-women. (I admit there is a problem here which gives the advantage to astronauts, but time and common sense and the public preference will sort it out.) And of course there are more and more amazing instruments for which the experts put together Greek and Latin names. But it is remarkable to what an extent the main features of each new venture are expressed in old familiar words—the launching pad, the count down, the blast off, the touch down, the lift off, the link up, the splash down—all these are made up of words our forbears have used for centuries, aided as usual by those stalwarts of English, the prepositions.

Neither jet nor rocket is a new word. Jet (from the French *jeter*, to throw) was used for a spurt of water in Tudor England, and rocket for a kind of firework (*rochetta*) brought from Italy at about that time. Nuclear science may be a modern growth, but *nucleus*, which in Latin meant the kernel of a nut, the very centre, was used in astronomy by Wren and Newton. Another word that has developed its scientific scope with the gradual expansion of man's knowledge is electricity. It comes from the Greek *elektron* which meant amber, the bright substance, for the root of the word was concerned with light. It was known from antiquity that amber had a strange magnetism that could be excited by friction, and centuries before this power was understood the word electricity was coined for it.

But it is to the simpler words of our own language that we turn most readily when we speak of the practical uses of modern inventions. We 'drive' a car as we would horses, we 'sail' in ocean liners without sails, and when we travel by air we 'fly' as if we were birds.

116

4 Naming the Arts

Of all the arts the one with the most distinguished name is music, derived of course from the nine Muses, the daughters of Zeus. It seems a little unfair that this one art should bear the name of all the nine, but if one examines their special provinces in detail, one finds that the arts as we think of them are not divided between them as we should do it. Seven of them are occupied with different kinds of poetry, song, drama and dance, all presumably involved with music, while the other two (Clio and Urania) look after history and astronomy. The visual arts—at which the Greeks so greatly excelled—have no part in the programme.

We still have no proper comprehensive word for painting, drawing and graphic design, and so we have taken to using the wider term, art, for all of these, which can be ambiguous. If you talk of artists you probably mean painters; if a girl goes to Art School it is to learn to paint. But 'painting' doesn't really cover the subject; it is a little too narrow, and art too wide. This is a curious gap in the language—not peculiar to English—especially curious when you consider the great antiquity of graphic art and the importance always attached to it. We don't know if the Stone Age men of 15,000 BC created music and drama (though we can confidently guess they did) but we do know from the caves of Lescaux that they were marvellous painters and draughtsmen.

If you try yourself to write a list of the principal 'fine arts' as we think of them now, you will find you are soon in difficulty. Music overlaps opera and ballet, which both overlap the theatre, which overlaps literature, which is an inadequate term, for it presupposes writing, and in all races people told stories and made poems long before they could write; and most early poems and tales were sung—which takes us back to music. No wonder the Muses' specialities seem a bit confused. But again we notice that the visual arts do not come into this circuit. They have a different circle of their own which links with the other only at the theatre; and just as there is no clear division between drawing and painting and between sculpture and architecture, so also there can be no hard line between words and music.

Let us turn to the new arts that have developed in this century, and first the cinema (Greek *kinema*, movement) in which sight and sound and ingenuity are combined together. I have called it by its most official name, but this is not its only name or even the one we use most, and the question of what posterity will chiefly call this art is still wide open.

The early inventors, competing with each other in producing new and improved systems, produced also a series of names to go with them on the usual Greek and Latin patterns of which Animatograph, Zoetrope, Kinetoscope, Photoscope, Cinematograph, Mutoscope, Biograph and Bioscope are a selection. Of these cinematograph, shortened to cinema, emerged as winner. But while the new art was still in its infancy the general public talked of it in more natural words, as they had of horseless carriages and flying machines, and their words were 'moving pictures'. The next step was to choose one of these two words. At first 'the pictures' seemed the favourite, then 'the movies' overtook it; but also in a more general way people began to speak of 'the screen', exactly as one talks of 'the stage', using the physical structure on which the art is displayed instead of an abstract name for the art itself. Then going one step further they began to call the pictures by another material name, that of the film on which they are printed. (Film is good Old English for a thin layer of anything.) No one could have foreseen that this substance would be singled out in this way, but at the moment it seems to be the public preference. 'A film star,' 'A film director,' 'Seen any good films lately?' This is what people are saying. But the subject is still fluid.

So we come to the youngest of the arts, television. The name, constructed on the usual plan, in this case Greek 'far' and Latin 'sight', seems satisfactory and has been generally accepted; but for something that has become literally a household word, almost as necessary to home life as a table or chair, it is just on the long side. Three syllables might pass but four is too much for the millions who say this word every day. So for most of them it is the telly or the TV.

We can see from other modern inventions that what starts colloquially can end up as the official name—as, for example, bus and taxi and van (which comes from caravan)—but in this case neither telly nor TV seems to qualify for promotion of this sort. Telly sounds too childish and TV is only an acronym.

Acronym itself is a new coinage, literally high name, the 'high' referring to the capital letters of which it is formed. I wrote 'only an acronym' deliberately for though we are bombarded with them on every side, see them in every newspaper, hear them in every news bulletin, and use them ourselves for convenience, yet they seldom seem to us like real words, only substitutes that are patently artificial. Used in moderation they are practical devices for saving time and space, but a heavy concentration of them can be stupefying.

We treat them inconsistently. Many being unpronounceable can never graduate as regular words, and in any case the majority refer to particular public organisations, often of a transitory nature, so that even if they are spoken as single words, as in the case of Nato and Nalgo, they can only be considered as proper nouns of uncertain duration rather than real additions to the general vocabulary. And even when it would be easy to say them as normal words, we have little inclination to do so. Much though we have heard of the TUC, for instance, over a long period, we never call it the Tuc (to rhyme with luck) or speak of tucism, as well we might.

However, the occasional acronym that can be easily spoken (possibly because its originators planned it so) and supplies a name for some important new thing—like radar (radio detection and ranging)—does qualify as a regular

119

common noun. This is certainly one method of creating new words and one that is on the increase, though not entirely new. There was, for instance, the original cabal in Charles II's time, which became a lasting word, though considered rather an oddity.

I suppose the most successful acronym of all time is the American-born OK, which is known to all the world. According to the OED, its origin is not the ignorant spelling 'Orl Korrect', as is sometimes said, but part of an election slogan used by a presidential candidate of the mid-nineteenth century who had been born at Old Kinderhook in New York State. It spread slowly through popular speech, taking its time to reach its zenith, and has now qualified as a regular word for we can write it with a small 'o' and treat it as verb or adjective. 'He okayed the plan and said it was quite okay.' Still slangy, perhaps, but that is no bar to advancement.

Workers in every profession habitually use the acronyms that belong to it, as part of the technical terms of their trade, which is my excuse for using OED so often in this book. But that doesn't mean that I claim word status for it. In conversation I should say Oxford Dictionary, or if relaxed among friends perhaps Oxford Dic. To most of us abbreviations come much more naturally than initials.

But to return to TV, already the public has found a name it likes better, one that is homelike and easy—the box. As yet it is used in a slightly jocular or even derogatory manner. 'I won't have the children staring at the box all day.' But it is surely coming and will I believe take its place beside the stage and the films and other familiar words that people have preferred to artificially made up ones. If you doubt that 'the box' can ever be taken seriously as the name of a profession or art-form, consider 'the stage' and 'the screen'. What is a stage but a raised platform of wooden boards? And then think of the significance the word had attained by Shakespeare's day and has maintained ever since; and that without losing its other uses, for there were landing stages on rivers, and at places where coaches stopped, as a convenience for passengers, and thereby it named the stage coach, and stages in life's journey. A stage is an ordinary wooden object and if it could rise in the realms of art, so can a box.

We see the same thing over and over again in regard to popular inventions. The Graeco-Latin name starts off with a good impetus and then gradually gives way to the choice of the people. Gramophone seemed very firmly fixed for a long time but then we started saying record-player which is actually longer but composed of our own words. Of course the word record is not of true English origin. Its root is the Latin *cor*, the heart, and to record something was to place it and keep it in one's heart, as Mary Tudor did with Calais. But although it came to us from Latin by way of French, it did so centuries ago, and since then we have used it in so many ways that it seems our own. Player is pure English.

Sporting records are deeply engraved on some people's hearts and can cause heartbreak too. How very different are the material objects of the musical world, the man-made discs on which sound has been captured and preserved. This is a specialised use of the word developed in English (for in French they are *disques*) and in this sense we use the word with precision, for although sound is also recorded on tapes we don't speak of them as records, except in a very general way. (We are always skilled at keeping different uses of the same word separate in our minds.) And tape is another Old English word (*tæppa*), like film (OE *filmen*), that has taken on exact new duties in modern technology.

The mention of discs could easily lead to a digression, for we have borrowed this word so often and in such different forms that it is quite an oddity: dish and desk in the Middle Ages (those early monks must have written at small round tables), and then, later, and more directly from the Latin, disc and discus. It has shown little tendency to go metaphorical, relating always to flat circular objects.

But to return to the matter in hand, the more we look into

121

this question, the clearer it seems to become that we like old familiar words better than artificially constructed new ones, and often choose to identify the new invention with a material object rather than an abstraction; also that it needs a long time to show if a new word has really taken root, and by then—with technology moving at the rate it does now—it may already be out of date.

One more point to remember is that though a word like gramophone is made of pure Greek, it isn't real Greek. It would puzzle Aristotle, and even modern Greeks don't use it. If you want a record-player in Athens now you must ask for a 'pickup'.

VII

THE LIVING LANGUAGE

1 Words are like People

Words are like human beings in the vagaries of fortune that may raise them up to great importance or cast them down. Of course their life span is very different from ours. Some indeed are stillborn, some popular for a season and then gone forever, but many have lived for over a thousand years and are still as vigorous as ever.

Apart from this little disparity they have much in common with ourselves. When grossly overworked they grow weak and feeble (awful is an obvious example), when totally neglected and forgotten they may actually die, for regular employment and exercise is as necessary for them as for us. But when nearly defunct they can rise up to a new life if some lucky chance revives them.

Such a chance came to the humble word budget, which in Middle English signified a leather bag for carrying odds and ends. It had many rivals, such as pouch, wallet, bag, pack and package, which all gained in favour while it sank out of use. By 1700 it was very old-fashioned. But in 1733 Sir Robert Walpole introduced in Parliament an unpopular bill on excise duties and a virulent political pamphlet likened him to 'a mountebank at a fair opening his budget of crank medicines'. From that moment 'budget' became linked in the public mind with methods of raising revenue and was thus launched on its political career. And not only political, for besides the Budget with a capital B for which the whole nation waits anxiously, the word has become a common noun, verb and adjective. We budget for this and that; we have budget shops and budget accounts. For a word that had nearly expired it is full of life and like its old rival, package,

123

which has found a new role in package tours, it is more prominent now than it ever was in its first occupation.

Another success story—almost a case of rags to riches—belongs to the word rubber. What this suggests first to any normal person today is the important raw material with its innumerable products that is known to hundreds of millions by this name. But until almost the end of the eighteenth century its regular meaning—apart from an obscure usage in some games—was of an object, perhaps a cloth or pad, that was used for rubbing something. Then came this strange, new substance from the East which proved to be efficacious for deleting pencil marks and was so used by artists who had formerly used pellets of bread for this purpose. Consequently it was a rubber, called at first Indiarubber to distinguish it from old-style rubbers, but gradually, as its other possibilities began to be realised, the India- was dropped and the simple task that provided its English name ceased to be thought of much account. When my small son, at school for a time in Canada, asked for a rubber to tidy up his drawing, his classmates shrieked with laughter for in their vocabulary what he wanted was an eraser and what he had asked for was an overshoe. He might have retorted, had he been more knowledgeable, by asking why they called their overshoes 'rubbers' if they were not made of the stuff that you rub out with.

A word that apparently died, defeated by foreign competition, but has risen again in part, is 'chapman'. In Old English it was the regular word for a buyer and seller of any kind of goods, a well-respected occupation. Then came the Normans with their French word *marchand*, now merchant, which was used for all important transactions so that the native chapman was left for lesser salesmen who finally took to the roads as mere travelling pedlars. Here too the word failed and faded except that it has left a plentiful crop of surnames showing how much it was once used. But it wasn't really dead. Shortened to chap, it lived on in slang, but at such a low level that for nearly a century it is hardly recorded. Then in this brief form, its commercial side forgotten, it began to float upwards as words often do from illiterate speech. Now it is right back, still very colloquial but pleasantly so, and much used. 'He's a good chap,' you say and can say it of anyone, though you still wouldn't use it in a formal piece of writing. But who knows? It may go on rising in status. Both 'boy' and 'girl' came up from colloquial speech and obscure origins.

Sometimes a word that once had a general meaning survives only in a narrow sense, like a man who once kept a large shop but now sells only bootlaces. Or maybe the word has found itself a number of specialised tasks to keep it going. Take, for instance, 'stall' which once meant a place, or rather the proper place for something to be in. We see this general meaning in the verb 'install'. If you have electricity installed it is put exactly where it is wanted. The verb 'stall' means to stick in one place and that is generally not so good. But the noun has survived only for a few very special places, and a comical mixture they are: a place for a cow to stand inside a shed, a seat for a choirboy or church dignitary in a cathedral, a seat in a theatre for those who have paid a good deal, a stand on which a vendor in the market or fête can set out his or her wares, and a shaped covering in which to put a sore finger. There are one or two more uses in industry, all with the idea of a container or compartment, but these I have detailed are the common ones. And note how exact they all are and unextendable. The stalls are only in one part of the theatre, and in the main body of a church no one can have a stall, not even if a grand chair is placed for him in the front row. This old word found its particular duties and sticks to them exactly.

Much of our English vocabulary is used with this precision. Our grammar is easy but our use of words highly idiomatic. It is as if they were long-established servants in a great household who discharge their duties to perfection but will not

125

touch those of another department (while others more easy-going might lend a hand with anything).

Think of the old English verb to play. In recent times it has been commercialised and many now play for their living, but the original idea of an activity indulged in for pleasure as a refreshment to mind or body is still well understood. However, the activities for which this word is used are strictly limited. We play all games but not field sports, and the line between them is finely drawn. You play polo but not show-jumping, even if it is a team event. You play cricket but not throwing the cricket ball or anything else. 'He plays the discus' is nonsense! We speak of the Olympic Games but you can't play running or jumping, still less 'play at' them. To say that would be an insult to the performers.

The reason lies far in the past. Running, riding, swimming, throwing, were all practical activities long before they were organised as sports, and only those sports whose origins lie in pure fun can use this word.

We also play music of all kinds. You can play a Beethoven sonata or a piano; or you can just play beautifully. But the usage here is different than it is with games. You play a violin but you don't play a racket or a bat. You play with a racket, but to say that Menuhin played with a violin would be dreadful. Likewise you can say that the musician's playing was masterly, but with a cricketer or tennis player it is his play that is brilliant or bad.

It is on the stage that the noun play comes into its own. Among all those grand words we have taken from the Greeks—theatre, drama, comedy and so on—the old English play still stands up strongly. If friends tell you they have been to a play you will be in no doubt about it; there can be no question that they might have gone to a concert, or a bridge party, or to watch tennis, though all these things are played. The actor still plays his part, from which we have the metaphor of playing one's part in any enterprise, though he is not called a player as often now as in Shakespeare's day.

But, strangely, you do not play ballet, and still less—in fact not at all—can you use this verb with any of the visual arts. To speak of playing a picture would be an absurdity, but it is hard to say why for painting is just as relaxing and refreshing to the spirit for those who have the gift for it as music is to the musician. It is nothing to do with hard work for no one works harder than the dedicated player of music. I think we must go back again, for an explanation, to the nine muses who did not include the graphic arts in their curriculum, and conclude that in primitive Europe painting and sculpture were undertaken more for practical ends than for pure pleasure. They were probably concerned chiefly with invoking magic, and magic was not a thing to play at.

I have not yet mentioned children's play because it has always been the same and raises no verbal problems. Children just play, or play at something or with something. You can hardly go wrong with their playing. But among older people what a versatile, subtle, difficult word it can be, though seeming so simple; it is full of the complications of human nature, and of pitfalls for the foreigner.

2 Daughters of Earth

Words are also like people in that they are sensitive, emotional, irrational and inconsistent. You could say it is we that have these qualities rather than the words, but we have made them, they express our feelings and their existence is bound up in ours. 'Words are the daughters of earth,' wrote Dr Johnson in the Preface to his Dictionary. He was quoting an earlier and more obscure writer but evidently concurred with the statement, which I take to mean that they are made by man and show his weaknesses as well as his better points.

Our way of life is changing now faster than ever before and this must be reflected in our speech. Our increased freedom of behaviour and abandonment of so many old conventions appears in the public and unembarrassed use of words that were formerly unmentionable in decent society. But as if to balance this we are now embarrassed by other words which formerly offered no problem. You must not, for instance, speak publicly of people being poor; they have to be underprivileged, deprived, disadvantaged or in a low income bracket. In speaking of a poor country the word is 'under-developed', or was until recently—for one of the drawbacks to euphemisms is that they are so short-lived. As soon as under-developed was established as meaning poor, it had to be changed to developing. Now it seems they are emergent.

Actually this nervousness about mentioning poverty began back in the last century but then it was only if the people concerned were within one's own circle of acquaintance. You could say guardedly that they were 'rather hard up' or 'not very well off' (what incredibly meaningless idioms when you look at the words individually, and yet their meaning was well understood). Or you could say 'in reduced circumstances'. Now it is the other way round. We tell people cheerfully how poor we are, and might say the same of our friends in a kindly way, but in regard to people we don't know, especially those actually starving in remote lands, we are careful to swathe our words in cotton wool. I believe we are much more considerate of other people's feelings than we used to be, and that can only be good, but it does produce a lot of verbal fluff.

It is a truly sad thing that the word coloured should have been so misused that it has come to be hated by those to whom it has been applied, so much so that many of them prefer to be called black. Jet black can certainly be beautiful, but on the whole this word has been too much associated with sadness and even wickedness for it to be a happy exchange. Besides, black is narrow and restricted compared to the glorious variety of all possible colour. The theme of colour has provided inspiration for many of our loveliest and most evocative words: crimson, scarlet, emerald, amethyst, azure, violet, amber, golden, russet, and so on. These are mostly metaphors drawing their beauty from the natural world—but their sounds are as lovely as the pictures they conjure up. Compared with colour, black is a sombre word, and white is worse for it is cold and negative. Colour can embrace us all, for we Europeans are not really white; it would be horrible if we were. If only we could all be called coloured and speak of the different races only by the lands they come from—as African or Indian or whatever. But that is not easy either, for people are apt to feel passionately about the names of countries, and some of them arouse so much feeling that they keep on changing. The names are difficult because people are difficult; but at the same time people can be fascinating and delightful—and so can words.

One thing about language is that it is so democratic, having no government but usage, and no laws but those we have evolved ourselves. And when I say 'we' I mean everyone from poets and professors to the most illiterate tramp, for the tramp's word may outlive the professor's. Unlike us the French do have an official body, the *Académie Française*, to lay down laws for their language, but it has little real control

over what they say. It is much opposed to the use of Fran-
glais—all those popular English words, le club, le sandwich
bar, le week-end, and so on—but is powerless to stop it. Such
a body if it were effective would constitute a verbal tyranny
whose effect would be more deadening than helpful.

We have had some examples lately here in England of
government interference with our speech and we dislike it
heartily. As weights and measures from the continent have
actually come into use, we are obliged to use the words that
belong to them. This is not the same as being told to call
a mile a kilometre, which we wouldn't do. But though we
have, for practical purposes, to measure in metres and kilo-
metres, the yard and the mile are still in our minds and I
would back them heavily to be still sometimes in our speech
a hundred years from now.

Then there is Women's Lib which is also trying to take
liberties with the language. Most people, I believe, are in
sympathy with the ideal of equal opportunity for both sexes,
but in making so much fuss about the long-established usages
of familiar words the organisers are leading their adherents
into deep waters, and are liable to distract attention from their
more serious aims. The word person, for instance, which they
use so much for want of anything better, is slightly comic
in itself, lacking the simple dignity of man or woman, and
coinages from it like chair-person sound silly. They are now, I
hear, seeking for something that can be used as a singular pronoun of common gender, and in this I wish them luck, for
there has always been a gap in the language here entailing the
awkward 'he or she', 'his or her'. But devising a new word
is one thing and getting more than a few enthusiasts to use
it is another. Whatever their efforts only the general public
of both sexes, and future generations, can give them success.

While there is no ultimate authority over language, there
have always been strong influences protecting it from too
much change, chiefly education, literature and entertainment, and this has always been so ever since children in

primitive tribes learned the legends and lore of their forbears from their elders and copied the sayings of their most admired leaders. There has also always been a strong desire among most people to communicate with others and have some social success. When someone speaks so uncouthly or strangely that he is not understood and gets little attention, he will make some effort to conform more nearly to the general speech.

When we look for the most outstanding influences on English in historic times the Authorised Version of the Bible must immediately come to mind. For at least four centuries, this was far and away the best-known book, not only in England but also in America and wherever the English settled all round the globe. An essential item for each family among the Pilgrim Fathers, it was also for many early colonists the only book they had. Generations were brought up to read it every day, and for thousands of primitive people taught by missionaries in more alien lands it provided the first introduction to English. By the nineteenth century much of its language was old-fashioned but none the less it formed a solid basis for the same ideal speech all round the world. This influence is now greatly weakened—almost gone, and in any case the original text has been so much adulterated lately that much of its compelling power is lost.

Among the scholars who stand out as great upholders of English we can't fail to think of Dr Johnson. His famous dictionary, published in 1755, the first of its kind, was indeed a milestone, quickly recognised by all who aspired to speak well as the final court of appeal for correct usage, spelling and pronunciation. But Johnson himself was too wise to take this view. He knew that a living language must always go on changing: 'May the lexicographer be derided,' he wrote, 'who shall imagine that his dictionary can embalm his language.... Sounds are too volatile and subtle for legal restraints': and he likened anyone who tried 'to enchain syllables' to one who would 'lash the wind'. All the same his

131

dictionary did provide a standard for good speech for a long time.

The next great landmark was the publication over many years (1884–1928) of the *Oxford English Dictionary* in thirteen large volumes, giving not only meanings but complete word histories as far as they can be known from ancient times. This has been the work of many scholars but first and foremost of Dr James Murray (later Sir James) who bore the main burden for thirty years and toiled even more arduously in his Oxford home than Johnson ever did in London. Neither received the support he deserved during the long work of preparation, but Murray had one advantage over Johnson in eleven children all brought up to help in the 'Scriptorium'— an annexe in his garden lined with thousands of paper-filled pigeonholes—from the time they could read. Johnson defined a lexicographer as 'a harmless drudge'; Murray whose immense learning (including twenty-five languages largely self-taught) far exceeded Johnson's, described himself as 'a nobody, a solar myth, an echo'. Anyone who cares for words must pay tribute to him and I like to think that perhaps he and Johnson can hobnob together in some lexicographer's paradise.

Murray knew well that his monumental work when published would not be final; nor can it ever be finished, for new editions, some shorter but more up to date, and supplements to the original continue to be issued and must go on. In fact all thinking people—except the few oddities like the promoters of Esperanto who think that a language can be artificially made—know that real languages are living organisms, which can indeed die as classical Latin has died, but while they live must constantly develop. And the grammarians and lexicographers are not so much referees blowing whistles as observers of the game, making careful notes on the way it is played.

Compilers of dictionaries must spend a large part of their time weighing up new possible entries for inclusion in the

132

next edition. It must be a dreadful task, for the borderline cases are often the kind of thing to make a sensitive scholar wince. The net of the OED is cast more widely now than ever before—acronyms, abbreviations and indecencies are included that would have appalled Dr Johnson and surprised Dr Murray, but however wide the net there must still always be doubtful cases. Is this one too commercial, that one too slovenly or too infantile? Which foreign words should be included? The editors make their own rules and abide by them impartially, never rejecting a word just because they dislike it. But we are not so bound. We have a free choice, and we are the ultimate arbiters of what will last.

But that small word 'we' includes several hundreds of millions, so what can we do about it? Only speak as well as we can, avoiding unnecessary Latinisms, worn-out clichés and useless padding. So let us not be motivated or activated at this moment of time into getting down to grass roots because, well, actually you know, it's just one of those things—I mean. Fortunately clichés are self-destroying. Ear-catching when first heard, they grow so tedious in repetition that new ones must be found, while the padding words (you know, sort of) that fill so many sentences are too uninteresting to have a lasting effect.

Many people are now despondent about the state of language both here in England and in America and elsewhere. In America the more enlightened of the population have coined the splendid word gobbledigook for the pompous jargon that afflicts so many public utterances. But lovers of English have often lamented its decline in the past. Dr Johnson deplored the importation of so many French words in his time, and how must the intelligent man of Anglo-Saxon stock have felt in the twelfth century? And yet the words most familiar to him and his forefathers have held their own triumphantly among the endless novelties that have been threatening to swamp them ever since, and they are still the ones we use most.

Words have amazing resilience and however much mal-treated they can survive unharmed for those who use them well. Such a one was Edward Thomas, killed in 1917, whose poem *Words* invokes them perfectly:

I know you:
You are light as dreams,
Tough as oak,
Precious as gold,
As poppies and corn,
Or an old cloak;
Sweet as our birds
To the ear,
As the burnet rose
In the heat
Of midsummer:
Strange as the races
Of dead and unborn:
Strange and sweet
Equally,
And familiar,
To the eye,
As the dearest faces
That a man knows,
And as lost homes are:
But though older far
Than oldest yew,—
As our hills are old,—
Worn new
Again and again:
Young as our streams
After rain:
And as dear
As the earth which you prove
That we love.

APPENDICES

1 Anglo-Saxon Poetry

Few people are familiar with Anglo-Saxon poetry because the archaic spelling and grammar with the sprinkling of obsolete words make it too difficult without serious study. Modernised versions must necessarily change some words entirely and alter others, which inevitably destroys the carefully balanced rhythm and alliteration on which the charm depends. But to give some idea of it, here is a short passage in which few of the words need much change, and so with a little contrivance both sense and sound can be kept close to the original. It comes from a sad poem called *The Wanderer* about a homeless man without leader or kindred. He dreams he is once more with his former lord, and lays on his lord's knee his hands and his head:

> Then a*w*akeneth again   the *w*anderer friendless,
> *s*eeth be*f*ore him   the *f*allow ways,
> *b*athing sea-*b*irds,   *b*roadening their feathers,
> *h*oar-frost and snow   with *h*ail a-mingled.
> Then are they *h*eavier   the wounds of the *h*eart,
> *s*ore after *s*weetness,   *s*orrow made new.

There is always a pause in the middle of each line (shown here by a space), and the alliteration (shown by italic letters) must come at the beginnings of strongly stressed syllables and link the two parts of the line together.

In case any reader is interested, here is the original:

> *Thonne onwæcneth eft   wineleas guma,*
> *ge-sith him beforan   fealwe wegas,*
> *bathian brimfuglas,   brædan fethra,*
> *hreosan hrim and snaw   hægle ge-menged.*
> *Thonne beoth thy hefigran   heortan benne,*
> *sare aefter swæsne,   sorg bith ge-niwad.*

Words that have disappeared completely and are here replaced with something unrelated are: *wineleas* (friendless), *guma* (man), *brim-* (the sea, but *fuglas* is the old form of fowls), *hreosan* (to fall), *benne* (wounds, *cf* bane) and *swæsne* (gentleness). *Hreosan hrim* could be translated 'frost-fall', but an h- was needed to alliterate with *hægle* (hail).

2 The Lord's Prayer

Translations from different periods illustrate some of the changes in the language.

1 Old English

Tenth century. From a translation of St Matthew's Gospel.

Faeder ure, thu the eart on heofonum,
Father   our, thou that art   in   heaven,

si thin nama ge-halgod.
be thy name   hallowed.

To-becume thin rice.
Come   thy rule.

Ge-wurthe thin willa on eorthan,
Be   done   thy will in   earth,

swa swa on heofonum.
as   also in heaven.

Urne ge-dæghwamlican hlaf gyf us to dæg.
Our   daily   loaf give us today.

And forgyf us ure gyltas
And forgive us our guilt

swa swa we forgyfath urum gyltendum.
as   also we forgive   our   guilty ones.

And ne ge-læd thu us on costnunge,
And not   lead thou us into trial,

ac a-lysus of yfele. Sothlice.
but release us from evil.   Soothly.

swa = so (see page 140)
daeg/hwam/lice = day/each/like, i.e. daily
costnunge = costing, i.e. evaluating or testing

2 Early Middle English
Thirteenth century. From *Reliquiae Antiquae*.

Fader oure that art in heve
i-halged bee thi nome.
I-cume thi kinereiche.
Y-worthe thi wylle also is in hevene so be on erthe.
Oure ich-dayes bred gif us to day,
& forgif us our gultes,
also we forgifet oure gultare,
& ne led us nowth into fondingge,
auth a-les ows of harme. So be hit.

This is still close to the Old English version, but the word order is changing, inflexions weakening, spelling erratic.

kinereiche = king-ric. *Cf* bishopric.
ich = each.
gultes = guilt (plural as in the Old English version).
fondingge = foolishness, a bad translation that did not last.
a-les (OE *a-lys*) is part of the verb 'loosen', to set free.

3 Late Middle English
Fourteenth century. From Wycliff's New Testament.

Oure fadir that art in heuenes,
halwid be thi name.
Thi kyngdom cumme to.
Be thi wille don as in heuen and in erthe.
Gif to vs this day ouer breed oure other substances,
and forgeue to vs oure dettis
as we forgeue to oure dettours,
and leede vs nat in to temptacioun,
but delyuere vs fro yuel. Amen.

4 *Early Modern English*
From Tyndale's Testament. 1526.

> O oure father which art in heven,
> halowed be thy name.
> Let thy kingdom come.
> Thy wyll be fulfilled, as well in erth
> as hit ys in heven.
> Geve vs this daye our dayly breade.
> And forgeve vs oure treaspases
> euen as we forgeve them which treaspas vs.
> Leede vs not into temptation,
> but delyvre vs from yvell. Amen.

The first of these versions is pure Anglo-Saxon, while the later ones bring in a few alien words, Wycliff being responsible for temptation and Tyndale for trespasses, and both concurring in the Hebrew Amen.

The Authorised Version, finished in 1611, followed Tyndale closely throughout the New Testament and those parts of the Old that he had completed. King James's bishops were working on this task at a peak period—some would say the peak—of the English language. They had a natural feeling for the music of words as well as for good scholarship and found both in Tyndale, supplementing his work with echoes of Wycliff and modifications of their own. The result was language that was already a little old-fashioned at that time, but of such high merit that it is sad to hear it supplanted even now.

Many of the most familiar passages of the Bible are Tyndale's work. Like Cranmer who composed the English Prayer Book he made an immeasurable contribution to the language, and also like him was burnt at the stake.

As to the spelling of these three versions of 'Our Father', it should be mentioned that Old English had some distinctive letters of its own for a few sounds, including 'th', that are not shown here. They can, however, be seen in Figure 1, appearing on page 66. It had no 'v', but a single 'f' between vowels was sounded like 'v', as in '*heofen*'. (The *-um* that ends it in this example is an inflexion showing it to be dative plural, i.e. in the heavens.) When 'v' was introduced by the Normans it was used interchangeably with 'u' and was no help at all but rather a hindrance for several centuries as may be seen in Wycliff's version.

A long 'a' in Old English has generally become a modern 'o', and the OE *swa* is the ancestor of our 'so' (the 'w' having fallen silent as it has in 'sword'). At a very early date the emphatic 'all so' was run together as 'also', and a further contraction produced 'as'. These have all survived as separate words which we use very variously, our common expressions 'so also', 'as also', 'so as', etc., being all sprung from the old *swa swa* which appears twice on page 137.

3 Our Commonest Words

While making the analysis of 4,000 words of ordinary talk as described on page 98, I was chiefly curious to see which words would appear as the most often used. But first I had to settle what to count as one word and at what point of variation it becomes a different one. A noun is obviously the same word whether singular, plural or possessive, and likewise I decided to treat a verb as one in all its parts (talk, talks, talked, talking) even in the case of the verb 'to be' which has eight very different forms. Pronouns posed a similar problem; 'I' and 'me' sound so different, but 'you' has no corresponding change, so for fairness' sake I took I/me/my together to balance against you/your, and similarly with the other pronouns. Again, with adjectives, I took old/older/oldest as variations of one word and that meant doing the same with good/better/best. It is only among our oldest and commonest words that these total changes of form occur.

There was also the problem of contractions, an outstanding feature of our conversation. Don't and can't seem like independent words, but when you come to I'm, I've, she'll, they're and so on, the possible variations are too numerous (Jim'll fix it) and I decided to treat them as if spoken in full. With these and other problems I tried to follow the usage of the dictionary and of common sense, and to avoid hairsplitting. There are no standard rules as to what is a word. An experimenter of this sort must make up his own.

When I had counted up all the words in my random specimen, I found that the top fifty were as given overleaf.

(to) be	238	up	23
the	205	(to) get	23
a/an	136	one	22
to	135	with	21
I/me/my	128	very	21
(to) have	120	(to) go	20
of	113	all	20
it	78	there	20
we/us/our	75	time	18
and	66	at	18
you/your	61	as	17
in	53	what	16
that	46	now	16
not	41	year	16
this/these	40	thing	15
they/them/their	39	will	15
(to) do	38	(to) make	15
on	34	more/most	15
he/him/his	33	if	14
(to) think	30	about	14
but	28	(to) know	14
can	27	here	14
well	26	who/whose	13
for	24	good/better/best	13
she/her	23	when	12

This may be thought a dull set of words. They are mostly structural, the nuts and bolts of English, all short, all (except 'very') Anglo-Saxon. Apart from 'thing', which is almost like a pronoun in use, only two nouns, 'time' and 'year', have got in among these top scorers. If I had had to guess the commonest nouns in the language, I would never have thought of these. But after all, time is the one element in our lives that affects every subject that we speak of. Whether it is politics, gardening, art or the family, phrases like this time, next time, just in time, last year, years ago, and so on are likely to come in, and so they did.

It may be noted that the top seven words together account for over a quarter of the total 4,000 spoken. But no one speaker would use them in this proportion. It is because they are common to *all* the speakers that they come so high. The verbs 'to be' and 'to have' owe their high scores chiefly to their use as auxiliaries to all other verbs, as also do 'can' and 'will'. 'Well' gets its numbers from the way in which most people begin their answer to a question with 'Well—'; while 'think' and 'know' represent the conversational 'I think' and 'You know'.

At the other end of the scale were nearly a thousand words that occurred only once each—mostly nouns, adjectives, and verbs of great variety and interest—and in between a mass of words of all kinds that scored between two and twelve. It was hard to know which one to put at the bottom of this list; fifty was a round number, and I could hardly stop at forty-nine, but in fact seven words were equal at twelve. I might have put in 'by', 'from' or 'any' (more nuts and bolts) or 'come', 'give' or 'look'. The next two nouns, at eleven each, were 'people' and 'house', but at this stage it was becoming like a traffic jam.

I am convinced that however many times one did a test of this sort, the giants (pigmy giants, for they are all small) would be always much the same; in the middle range there would be some fluctuation, but the last thousand or so, occurring only once or twice each, would be endlessly different, for the possibilities of what might be spoken are almost infinite.

INDEX

Pilgrim Fathers, the, 45, 131
pilgrimages, 48–9
place-names, 5, 42, 45, 52
Polynesia, loan-words from, 84
printing, importance of, 68–9, 72

Renaissance, the, 65, 86
rhyming, 11, 16
Rivers, Anthony Woodville, Earl, 68
Romance languages, 45, 93
Roman Empire, the, 44, 54
  and Britain, 54–5
Russian language, 23, 36

Sanscrit, 36
Scandinavia, 8, 36, 61, 93
scientific terms, 74, 86, 109, 116
Scotland:
  Gaelic of, 91–2
  Scots English in, 37, 39
Scott, Sir Walter, 92, 103
Shakespeare, William, 72–3, 83, 91, 94
Sir Gawain and the Green Knight, 67
slang, 14, 86

Slavonic languages, 36
Spanish language, loan-words from, 85
Stone Age, the, 2, 8, 117

television, 65, 72, 118–20
theatre, the, 72, 126
Thomas, Dylan, 95–6
Thomas, Edward, 96, 134
Times, The, 96, 98
transport:
  by air, 115–16
  by car, 112–14
  by rail, 111
Tyndale, William, 139

Vedas, the, 36

Wales, and Saxon invasion of Britain, 52
Walpole, Sir Robert, 123
Welsh language, 36, 42, 89–91
Wodehouse, P. G., 96
Women's Lib, 130
Wycliff, John, 138–9